Puccini

His Life and Music

www.naxos.com/naxosbooks/puccinilifeandmusic

by Julian Haylock

Puccini
His Life and Music

Author's Acknowledgements

Any work of this kind is by its very nature an accumulation of collective wisdom gleaned from a wide variety of sources over a long period of time, although I would like to pay tribute to the late Julian Budden, whose insatiable enthusiasm and encyclopaedic knowledge of Puccini's life and work were inspirational. Of the many distinguished artists I have been privileged to meet over the years, Lorin Maazel and Zubin Mehta are specially significant for their robust defence of Puccini's music at a time when such passionately held opinions were deeply unfashionable. Heartfelt thanks also to Genevieve Helsby and her team for their expertise and tireless support, and to Barbara and Stephanie for happily journeying with me during my 'Puccini year'.

Published by Naxos Books, an imprint of Naxos Rights International Ltd

© Naxos Books 2008

www.naxosbooks.com

Printed and bound in China by Leo Paper Group

Design and layout: Hannah Davies, Fruition – Creative Concepts

All photographs © Lebrecht Music & Arts Photo Library

Front cover background picture: Set design for Act III Scene 1 of *Turandot* by Emil Preetorius, Nürnberg, 1942

A CIP Record for this book is available from the British Library.

ISBN: 978-1-84379-230-7

Contents

www.naxos.com/naxosbooks/puccinilifeandmusic

Visit the dedicated website for *Puccini: His Life and Music* and gain free access to the following:

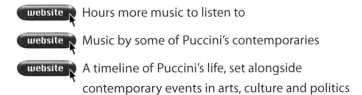

Hours more music to listen to

Music by some of Puccini's contemporaries

A timeline of Puccini's life, set alongside contemporary events in arts, culture and politics

To access this you will need:

- ISBN: 9781843792307
- Password: Butterfly

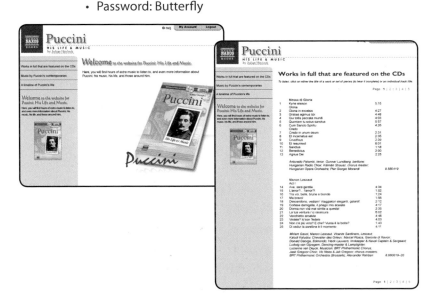

www.naxos.com/naxosbooks/puccinilifeandmusic

Introduction

Giacomo Puccini was the last major figure in the 300-year-old tradition of Italian opera composers which began so spectacularly with Claudio Monteverdi. He had the good fortune to emerge during the 1890s just as Giuseppe Verdi – fêted composer of *Rigoletto*, *Il trovatore*, *La traviata* and *Aida* – was nearing the end of his long and illustrious career. The way was clear for someone to inherit Verdi's mantle and carry it into the next century: the emotional intensity of Puccini's music seemed to fill the void created by the older man's retirement.

For three centuries Italy had proved to be a crucible for the development of opera. In *Orfeo*, premiered in 1607, Claudio Monteverdi (1567–1643) built on the experiments of members of the Florentine Camerata – notably Peri (1561–1633) and Caccini (1551–1618); he achieved a magical synthesis of words and music: madrigal, lute song and all manner of new orchestral sonorities combined with linear plot development to make a compelling theatrical entertainment. Opera continued to play a vital role in Italian musical life during the eighteenth century. *Opera seria*, which often drew on the work of the prolific Italian poet and librettist Pietro Metastasio (1698–1782), was a genre of formalised music drama in which the plot, usually derived from classical mythology, was advanced by the performers singing 'recitatives'; these were interspersed with arias reserved for the expression of single, basic emotional reactions to developments in the plot. As a reaction against these earnest machinations there emerged the more light-hearted style of *opera buffa*. This was a frothy concoction designed to raise the spirits, as exemplified by the music of Pergolesi (1710–1736) – whose *La serva padrona* (1733) virtually defined the genre – together with Paisiello (1740–1816) and Cimarosa (1749–1801).

For Italians during the nineteenth century, opera became not so much a way of life as a religion in which composers and singers were worshipped as gods. Leading the way was one of the most ebullient and indestructible musical personalities ever to flourish a composing pen: Gioachino Rossini (1792–1868). Whether in comic operas such as *Il barbiere di Siviglia* ('The Barber of Seville', 1816) – Verdi deemed it 'the finest *opera buffa* ever composed' – or in serious works such as *Guillaume Tell* (1829), Rossini's melodic fecundity was inexhaustible, the speed at which he composed unrivalled.

Gaetano Donizetti (1797–1848) and Vincenzo Bellini (1801–1835) were the most gifted of Rossini's younger contemporaries. Between 1816 and 1844 Donizetti produced an astonishing seventy operas which, if somewhat uneven in quality, feature at least three unassailable masterpieces: *L'elisir d'amore* ('The Elixir of Love', 1832), *Lucia di Lammermoor* (1835) and *La Fille du régiment* ('The Daughter of the Regiment', 1840). In the tragically short time available to him Bellini advanced the *bel canto* style of vocal writing, in which vocal agility, brilliance and pearly smoothness are prized above all else.

With the emergence of Giuseppe Verdi (1813–1901), Italian opera was to move into new realms of musico-dramatic sophistication and political engagement. Operas such as *Nabucco* (1842) inspired the unifying partisans of

Risorgimento Italy with symbols of a country's struggle against foreign domination; Verdi plumbed new depths of characterisation in *Rigoletto* (1851) and *La traviata* (1853); he nodded at French Grand Opera in *Aida* (1871); and after a thirteen-year break from opera, he resurfaced in his late seventies to present two unequivocal masterpieces based on plays by Shakespeare – *Otello* (1887) and *Falstaff* (1893). Rather than looking back, in musical terms these last two operas represent further technical advances: Verdi used extended melodic writing – beyond the formal structures of recitative, aria and ensemble – to develop a more through-composed style capable of embracing and sustaining the disparate emotions inherent in both comedy and tragedy. It was this supreme development of the Italian operatic tradition that paved the way for the composer who would extend it into the twentieth century: Giacomo Puccini.

Unlike Verdi, Puccini quickly discovered that depicting events on an epic scale was not his forte; he concentrated instead on the kind of personal or domestic intrigues that hold soap-opera audiences spellbound today. He was an instinctive melodist–harmonist whose solo set-pieces are invariably built out of short, repeated phrases, soaring higher and higher, driven by chains of poignant harmonic suspensions. If his emotional range is more limited than Mozart's, Verdi's or Wagner's, he is unsurpassed when it comes to expressing feelings associated with falling in love – something to which he himself was prone all too often. He depicts neither epic nor erotic love but rather an idealised intimacy and purity which – when threatened or betrayed – has tragic and sometimes violent consequences.

Puccini was sensitive to the new realism that was then dominating Italian opera: the popular term for it was *verismo*, meaning 'true to life'. The genre, in effect instigated by

Mascagni's enormously successful one-act opera *Cavalleria rusticana* (1890), transformed 'kitchen-sink' or 'low-life' subjects into operatic dramas. In addition to exploring accessible (rather than mythical) subject matters, veristic operas used melodramatic plots through which composers expressed extremes of emotion, sometimes violently. Puccini, often considered a composer of the *verismo* school, was not strictly speaking so. Rather, the *verismo* movement inspired him to use different features of its style in a number of his works. His three most celebrated operas – *La Bohème* (1896), *Tosca* (1900) and *Madama Butterfly* (1904) – are masterpieces of emotional timing and manipulation that grab an audience by the scruff of the neck, leaving its collective sensibilities in tatters by the end. Only Tchaikovsky, Janáček, Berg and Britten might be said to have so fearlessly negotiated such harrowing emotional terrain.

In the first decade of the twentieth century Puccini found himself on the receiving end of a critical onslaught launched by the Italian avant-garde, with *verismo* – and indeed all opera – as its target; in later generations he has also come in for criticism, which strikes modern opera-lovers, with their eclectic listening habits, as rather snobbish. But even Puccini's detractors invariably concede that he possessed a rare instinct for dramatic pacing. He was a perfectionist in all things, and struggled throughout his life to find suitable opera librettos that matched up to his high standards. He integrated every element of music, words and gesture, ensuring that each scene moved with complete naturalness and believability. Puccini shared Wagner's concern for the totality of the scenic concept, but in contrast to the monumentality of Wagner's music Puccini's glides by with a sleight-of-hand nonchalance. He speaks with the voice of the people, concentrating on heightened sentiment rather than global or metaphysical tragedy. As the critic Julian Budden remarks, 'His values were those of "L'italietta", the bourgeois, unadventurous Italy before World War I. "Great sorrows in little souls" was his watchword.'

Anticipating the techniques used by Hollywood film composers, whereby music passes seamlessly from foreground to background in harmony with the emotional temperature and topography of the scenes, Puccini timed his music for maximum impact, fine-tuning it to the natural rhythms of stagecraft. As he once memorably put it, 'A curtain raised or dropped too late often means the failure of an opera.' He also claimed – with some justification – that his operas could be sung in any language and still be clearly understood. The celebrated conductor Arturo Toscanini (who conducted the premiere of *Turandot* in 1926) put it rather less kindly – 'In many Puccini operas you could change the words and any other set would do' – while the Russian composer Dmitry Shostakovich came up with the ultimate put-down, in conversation with Benjamin Britten: 'Puccini wrote marvellous operas, although his music is dreadful'.

Puccini was the first Italian opera composer whose orchestral writing kept pace with the European mainstream. Although his later work was influenced by the luminescent textures and Eastern spice of Ravel and Debussy (whose *Pelléas et Mélisande* he admired for its 'extraordinary harmonic qualities and most delicate instrumental effects'), he was temperamentally closer to the post-Romantic aesthetic of Rachmaninov. Puccini shared with Wagner the use of a particular musical technique: the 'leitmotif' (leading motif), a musical 'tag' attached to a character, an idea, a feeling or an object. Compared to the rigour with which Wagner applied the technique, Puccini's use of motifs was looser; but they do prompt memories of previous scenes and incidents, as well as bind the music together and give it emotional energy.

Unlike some of his contemporaries, Puccini knew that he could achieve his goals without recourse to inventing a new musical language. He considered Stravinsky's epoch-making ballet *The Rite of Spring* 'the creation of a madman' (for his part the Russian dismissed *Madama Butterfly* as 'treacly violin music'); and Puccini was appalled to hear Richard Strauss instruct an orchestra to 'make a noise like a menagerie' (Strauss meanwhile complained that he couldn't tell the difference between *La Bohème* and *Madama Butterfly*). Puccini was not an instinctive intellectual and considered art 'a kind of illness'.

Following an initial wave of back-to-back masterpieces, Puccini's production rate slowed significantly as he sought fresh challenges that would help him refine and hone his technique. One senses this especially in the music of *La rondine* (1917): it may lack the emotional clout of its predecessors (despite its consummate skill and conversational fluency), yet the opera's iridescent musical surfaces make this arguably the jewel in Puccini's crown.

Puccini's operas continue to play to sell-out houses all over the world, and yet the critical fraternity has remained decidedly aloof. In his widely read book *Music Ho!* (1934), the English composer and conductor Constant Lambert curtly dismissed Puccini's music as 'vulgarised', while in his *Art of Judging Music* (1948) the American composer and educator Virgil Thomson put the academic perspective in a nutshell:

> *Puccini's operas have probably the lowest intellectual content of any, although their plots are far from stupid. Their expressive content, which is chiefly self-pity, is powerful by its simplicity. But the emotional composition of this has little*

depth or perspective, and the musical textures employed are
of small interest as workmanship.

Today, however, there is no shortage of critics willing to take
up the cudgels in Puccini's defence. Denis Forman asserts that
'no criticism can touch Puccini today. *La Bohème*, *Tosca*, and
Butterfly ride the opera houses of the world and they have
become the engines that drag behind them the lesser operas
of yesterday and the unpopular operas of today.'

Away from composing, what kind of man was Puccini?
Perhaps he might best be summed up by that old-fashioned
expression, 'a man's man'. He adored women (and they him),
and he was handy with both shotgun and fishing rod. Speed
was something of an obsession too, resulting in a succession of
cars and boats. His string of adulterous affairs and his passion
for blasting ducks out of the sky may make him a somewhat
less than sympathetic character today, even if such attitudes
were far from untypical in his time.

What endures, of course, when dust has returned to dust
and ashes to ashes, is the musical legacy. Puccini's is not in
doubt – check the schedules of any opera company in the
world, and one name virtually guaranteed not to be absent is
that of Giacomo Puccini. At the end of his life Puccini himself
put everything in perspective: 'Almighty God touched me with
his little finger and said: "Write for the theatre – mind, only
for the theatre." And I have obeyed his supreme command.'

Chapter 1

From Lucca to Milan

From Lucca to Milan

Giacomo Antonio Domenico Michele Secondo Maria Puccini was the right man born in the right place at the right time. Descended from four generations of gifted composers and organists, he was given every opportunity as a child to develop his talent. Yet he didn't hit the ground running. Rather he honed his burgeoning creative skills over a number of years. Puccini was twenty-five before he discovered that opera was his true métier and thirty-seven when he produced his first indisputable masterpiece: *La Bohème*. When international fame finally beckoned, he was well and truly prepared.

The composer was born in Lucca, Tuscany, on 22 December 1858, the fifth of seven children to Michele and Albina Puccini. Michele was forty-five years old and a well-established musician in Lucca – a former Roman colony famous for its architecture, defensive outer walls, tree-crested Guinigi Tower, narrow winding streets, and colossal amphitheatre. Michele's teachers had included Saverio Mercadante (1795–1870) and Donizetti, and he had upheld the family tradition by becoming organist and choirmaster at the Cathedral of San Martino.

As part of his responsibilities Michele composed a series of attractive religious works, but of special significance was his opera *Giambattista Cattani* (1844) which created quite a stir in Lucca at the time. Michele died when Puccini was only five years old, yet the young boy's musical destiny was already mapped out for him. Michele's brother-in-law, Fortunato Magi, temporarily assumed responsibility for the music at San Martino on the legally binding condition that as soon as Puccini was 'able to discharge such duties', Magi would stand aside.

Although Michele's influence on his son proved to be short-lived, Puccini's mother, the indomitable thirty-two-year-old Albina, did everything in her power to bring him up in the family mould. This proved to be something of an uphill struggle at times as Puccini was not the most willing or industrious of students. According to his sister Ramelde:

> *Giacomo was endowed with a very lively mind and a sensitive heart. But the darling boy, perhaps because of his extraordinary vitality and restlessness of character, refused to take an interest in any kind of study... Although he loved his mother deeply, Giacomo was no good at sitting long at a school desk and was frequently expelled to be readmitted only through his mother's petitions.*

Puccini's first singing and organ lessons with Magi proved rather underwhelming, but matters improved dramatically with a change of teacher to Carlo Angeloni – a rather dour former pupil of Michele's – at the local Pacini Musical Institute. By his tenth birthday Puccini was a chorister at both San Martino and San Michele; his keyboard skills were such that by his mid-teens he was performing and extemporising regularly as organist at San Martino and several other churches in the Lucca area.

Music came naturally to Puccini – it was in his genes. It also paid relatively well, and in order to help his mother make ends meet he began playing the piano in local taverns (barely disguised brothels), just as Brahms had done in the backstreets of Hamburg a quarter-century earlier. But whereas the ultra-sensitive Brahms carried the mental scars of his experiences with him for the rest of his life, Puccini had an outward-going, urbane side to his nature that painlessly carried him through.

Puccini was an early smoker and part of the money he earned was secretly held back to sustain the habit. Piano-playing wasn't his only source of cigarette money, however. With the help of some friends he began stealing organ pipes and selling them on, cleverly obfuscating the fact by avoiding the 'missing' notes when playing in church. Another aspect of his relationship with the 'king of the instruments' (Mozart's description of the organ) which brought him into disrepute was his habit of introducing themes from popular operas – Verdi's were particular favourites – into his extemporisations. Under Angeloni's instruction, Puccini had made an in-depth study of the master's *Il trovatore*, *La traviata* and *Rigoletto*, and it seems that at times his enthusiasm simply overcame him in the organ loft.

It was around this time that Puccini began composing. In 1875 he produced a number of simple, short organ pieces by way of experimentation as well as his earliest vocal setting, a song for mezzo-soprano and piano entitled 'A te' ('To You'). Listeners will search this innocent little pleasantry in vain for premonitions of 'Nessun dorma', but at least the tremolando coda carries with it an unmistakable sense of the dramatic. Up until now Puccini had viewed composing as little more than functional – the organ pieces had in part been composed as exercises for a young pupil – but this was soon to change.

Puccini was born into a musical world in which Verdi reigned supreme: at that time *Aida* was the hottest ticket in town. When at last Puccini had the opportunity to witness this musical phenomenon at first hand, there was no stopping him. On 11 March 1876 he set off on foot with two friends to make the twenty-kilometre journey to Pisa to see his first-ever professional opera production. Despite having neither ticket nor money he somehow managed to bluff his way in and what he saw there changed his life for ever. 'When I heard *Aida* at Pisa,' he recalled, 'I felt that a musical window had opened for me.' From that day forward, Puccini's sights became firmly fixed on Milan, the nerve-centre of Italy's operatic world.

Puccini in 1876, aged 18

First, however, the seventeen-year-old organist-cum-composer had to make up for lost time. Before entertaining the idea of producing a full-scale opera there was the not inconsiderable matter of learning some basic orchestral technique. It is hardly surprising, therefore, that his one major work of 1876 was the *Preludio a orchestra*, dated 5 August; for many years it was considered lost, until in 1999 the city of Lucca acquired the original ten-page manuscript from an anonymous private collector. Considering this was Puccini's first attempt at such a work, the two-and-a-half-minute miniature packs quite a punch. Shades of Mendelssohn and Schubert colour the E minor opening, while there is more than a hint of Delibes in the upper string tremolandos. Despite its structural diffuseness, it is above all a powerful artistic statement of intent which went far beyond anything he had so far produced.

Contemporary records indicate that the *Preludio* went unperformed, yet Puccini's next work just a few months later, the *Mottetto per San Paolino*, received two public airings in 1877 – first at the Pacini Institute (where Puccini was still a student) and then in the church of San Paolino itself. The *Mottetto*, scored for baritone solo, mixed chorus and orchestra, is a more confident assertion of Puccini's burgeoning creative powers. Here the accent is more indelibly Italian (and Verdian), even if Gounod hovers in the background. The orchestra-and-chorus bookends pay unmistakable homage to the Grand March from *Aida* which had so stirred Puccini's senses the previous year.

Composed around the same time, the cantata *Cessato il suon dell'armi* for tenor solo, chorus and orchestra was thought lost until as recently as 2003, when Puccini's granddaughter Simonetta made a surprise announcement that some of the original parts had survived and were in her possession. This exuberant seven-minute piece was taken into the recording studios in June 2003 by conductor Riccardo Chailly as part of an invaluable collection of Puccini rarities.

Almost exactly a year after its premiere the *Mottetto per San Paolino* received a repeat performance in the eponymous church as part of a composite Mass setting by pupils at the Pacini Institute. Puccini contributed a new Credo, the most confidently handled, structurally integrated and naturally flowing of his pieces so far. A review of the time talks of its 'original touches' and 'maturity', and although anyone coming to it unprompted would almost certainly name Verdi as its composer, the fact that it passes muster as the work of an experienced professional is a fair indication of Puccini's achievement.

The only other work of the 1870s to have survived is another choral piece, *Vexilla regis*, for two-part male choir and organ. There is no record of a performance of this brief, ternary-form setting of the Latin Passiontide hymn, and in fairness nothing here suggests that the piece's composer would go on to produce some of the most cherished works in the Italian operatic tradition. This was clearly as much a time of consolidation for Puccini as it was a chance to experiment with new ideas.

As Puccini fast approached the end of his formal training at the Pacini Institute, he was keen to experience the bright lights of Milan. In a relatively short space of time he had pulled away from the pack to become the most promising composer Lucca had produced in years. Before leaving, however, he had his graduation piece to compose: a *Messa a quattro voci* (1880) which incorporated the 1878 Credo and (in between the Gloria and Credo) the 1877 *Mottetto*. Premiered during the Feast of San Paolino with a performance time of around forty-five minutes, this was by far the largest work Puccini had produced, and it proved something of a triumph. Remarkably, nothing more was heard of it until 1951, when Dante Del Fiorentino, a priest who had known Puccini during his student years, discovered the original manuscript while researching a biography of the composer; he submitted it for publication under the spurious title *Messa di gloria*. The musical world was gently stirred rather than shaken by its sudden reappearance, but for Puccini lovers it provided the vital missing link between the small-scale apprentice pieces of the 1870s and the composer's initial bids for operatic stardom.

When listening to the *Messa a quattro voci* it is as well to remember that Italian choral music had its own unique flavour. For the heirs of J.S. Bach, Haydn, Mozart, Schubert and Beethoven working in the Austro-German heartlands, religious composition was a solemn business – as it was in Russia, Scandinavia, Bohemia and Victorian Britain. Among French composers, even opera supremo Charles Gounod had done little more than gently loosen the stylistic bonds in his Masses, to a chorus of general disapproval from traditionalists. In notoriously insular Italy, however, the major precedents for large-scale religious works were operatic hybrids. So when Puccini set to work on his five-movement Mass the music he would have had ringing in his ears would most likely have been Rossini's *Stabat mater* and *Petite Messe solennelle*, the sacred music of Bellini and Donizetti, and most especially Verdi's all-embracing *Messa da Requiem* – composed only six years earlier.

Puccini's *Messa* represents a creative leap for the budding young composer. This is evident right from the start of the piece, with its contrapuntal, overlapping string writing which segues into the choir's 'Kyrie eleison'. Puccini thought so much of this passage that he later incorporated it into his second opera, *Edgar*. Only in the dramatic, central 'Christe eleison' does Verdi's influence unmistakably make itself felt. The codetta's gently falling chromaticisms over a held bass note are strangely reminiscent of Borodin, yet the overriding feature of this music is its ease and sincerity of expression. For the first time, a piece by Puccini has the potential to make the hairs at the nape of the neck stand on end.

The Gloria moves us into a world of overt melodrama, with its propensity for secular earthiness rather than sacred dignity. Alongside that of Verdi is the influence of Gounod, whose opera *Faust* was one of the few 'foreign' operas that Italians had taken to their collective bosom. The 'Gratias agimus te' section features Puccini's most eloquent tenor solo to date, while the final 'Cum sancto spiritu' demonstrates that he had also become skilled in fugal composition. The imposing

Credo, composed two years earlier, rather overwhelms the gentle Sanctus, which lasts a mere three-and-a-half minutes. A phrase in the Benedictus was to re-emerge in the second-act minuet of *Manon Lescaut* (Puccini's third opera), while the lightweight Agnus Dei finale was lifted wholesale for the same opera's madrigale section (where it sounds a great deal more convincing). Yet for all that, the *Messa a quattro voci* demonstrated that in the space of just two years Puccini had risen from being a provincial to a national talent. The time was right for him to move to the country's most celebrated operatic metropolis: Milan.

First, however, funds had to be raised for three years of advanced study at the Milan Conservatoire. This was far beyond the means of his immediate family, so Puccini's mother, the ever-resourceful Albina, petitioned the city council for financial support. The council refused on three separate occasions, even when Puccini himself interceded. It has been suggested that he might have put official noses out of joint with his irascible teenage behaviour; it seems more likely, however, that since Puccini was effectively turning his back on Lucca by refusing the family post at the Cathedral of San Martino, it was felt that he could now pay his own way. Smarting from the authorities' lack of support, Albina went straight to the top – to Queen Margherita, no less, who held the purse-strings of a fund set up specially to help gifted students from poor backgrounds. The Queen granted enough money to cover a year's full fees, and then a paternal uncle (a medical doctor named Nicolau Cerù) stepped in and guaranteed the balance. At last, Puccini was on his way.

On his arrival in Milan, Puccini began to breathe the air of a different planet. Here was the world-famous Teatro alla Scala, the performing hub of Italian music which put on productions of the highest standard featuring internationally famous artists. Verdi led the way with *Aida* (by some margin) and *Rigoletto*; Rossini and Donizetti were the favoured older composers; more recent compositions sprang from the pens of Amilcare Ponchielli (1834–1886) and Alfredo Catalani (1854–1893), alongside French imports Gounod, Massenet, Halévy, Adam, Thomas and Bizet. Puccini immersed himself in opera as never before, revelling in its intoxicating fusion of poetic intimacy and raw emotional power.

By comparison, chamber and orchestral works were viewed by most Italians as a sideline rather than a core necessity. Incredibly, when Puccini first entered the Milan Conservatoire in the autumn of 1880, there had never been a public performance of a symphony in Lucca. But even if opera remained at the centre of Italian musical life, the spread of Wagnerian ideology had necessitated a rethink as to the importance of the pit orchestra. Hitherto, Italian opera orchestras had often been relegated to providing little more than 'rum-ti-tum' accompaniments for the stratospherics of coloratura sopranos, but they were now an increasingly vital part of the musical fabric. Wagner's concept of the *Gesamtkunstwerk* ('total art-work') placed equal emphasis on each separate element of opera – music, words, drama and scenery; and he used leitmotifs as building-blocks in his opera music, which flowed seamlessly and organically rather than comprising a sequence of 'numbers' (overtures, recitatives, arias and ensembles). Puccini would later draw on Wagner's use of motifs in his own compositions, but at this juncture the impact of Wagner's actual music – as opposed to his ideas – had been minimal, at least in Italy. The first performance of a Wagner opera on the peninsula, *Lohengrin* (not the easiest listening experience for the uninitiated, although in the main the Italians loved it), had occurred as recently as 1871 in Bologna.

Milan was providing orchestral concerts focusing on light music and virtuoso showpieces, but symphonies remained the exclusive concern of the Conservatoire. Here Puccini began to immerse himself in the cultural sea-change. His first stroke of luck was in having as his tutor Antonio Bazzini (1818–1897) – composer of that hilarious cornucopia of violin pyrotechnics *La Ronde des lutins*. Bazzini was fully versed in the theatrical side of music, and had himself produced an (unsuccessful) opera entitled *Turanda* in 1867. He was pro-Wagner, so Puccini had easy access to Wagner's latest scores; yet Bazzini's heart was really in instrumental music. As a result, Puccini was encouraged to compose a series of student pieces for string quartet. For the Romantic composer – and Puccini fitted into this category – the string section was the orchestra's engine, its emotional powerhouse, its very soul. If the budding orchestrator could master string technique, half the battle was already won.

With its playfully exaggerated upbeats the principal material in the first movement of a planned string quartet in D major sounds like pure Haydn, while its more lyrical second subject suggests familiarity with Mendelssohn's set of three quartets, Op. 44. Mendelssohn is also the starting point for the Scherzo in A minor (without trio), a two-and-a-quarter-minute charmer that breathes a life all its own, replete with Hispanic arabesques. Another Scherzo, in D minor and also without trio, possesses a passion and forward drive more reminiscent of Mendelssohn's early string symphonies. Never one to waste a good idea, Puccini would reappropriate it as the introductory waltz in his first opera, *Le villi*. The last of these preparatory pieces for string quartet – a set of three minuets and trios in A major – dates from 1884, the year in which *Le villi* first saw the light of day. These pieces have the relaxed bonhomie of Antonín Dvořák (1841–1904); the minuets, both gracefully and idiomatically scored, are gloriously uncomplicated and upbeat.

Puccini produced a set of three keyboard fugues in the Baroque manner at various times between 1880 and 1883, merely as pedagogical exercises. No one could possibly guess their composer – the G and A major pieces are unashamedly Mendelssohnian, while the C minor sounds like a refugee from Bach's *Art of Fugue* – and yet Puccini's ability to breathe warmth and humanity into even the most intricate of contrapuntal textures shines through. These are skilfully wrought miniatures that one can listen to with pleasure.

Puccini appears to have embraced life at the Conservatoire with alacrity. After just two lessons with Bazzini, in December 1880 he wrote excitedly to his mother:

> *I have made myself this timetable: in the morning I get up at half-past eight and when I have a lesson I go to it. If I have no lesson I practice the piano a little. I don't need to do too much, but I have to practice a bit... I go on until half-past ten; then I have lunch and go out. At one I come home and work for a couple of hours preparing for Bazzini, then from three to five at the piano again for some reading of classical music.*

Each day ended in style with a cheap meal, half a litre of wine, a cigar, a long walk, then bed with a novel.

Puccini also mentioned that he was studying *Mefistofele*, the 1868 opera by the librettist, composer, poet and critic Arrigo Boito (1842–1918). It was Boito who had recently written the libretto for *La Gioconda* (1876) by Ponchielli, the composer who would become Puccini's main teacher at the

Conservatoire. Within a year of Puccini's letter of 1880, Boito would complete the first of three collaborations with Verdi, *Simon Boccanegra* – to be followed towards the end of Verdi's life by *Otello* and *Falstaff*.

Money was always in short supply, so much so that Puccini was forced to change address frequently to help make ends meet. He seems to have applied himself satisfactorily to composition, although by the spring of 1881, according to a letter from Bazzini to Albina, Puccini's other music studies were giving cause for concern.

Amilcare Ponchielli

Your son Giacomo is doing well and making progress in his principal study of composition. He has been somewhat neglectful of his subsidiary studies (piano, aesthetics, dramatic theory, etc.) despite repeated urgings from me and for this there are penalties to be paid... he really must convince himself (and I have told him so) that the Academic Council does not make exceptions *and that* all the courses must be followed.

During one excruciatingly dull lesson Puccini had written in a book: 'Oh God! Help! Goodbye, Professor, I'm going to sleep, I'm dying!' Yet the overall impression is of a likeable person with much promise but somewhat lacking in intellectual resolve.

Like most young men of twenty-five, Puccini found life in the metropolis too full of tempting distractions to want to closet himself away from all the fun. Despite his obvious ability, he was essentially a down-to-earth sort who preferred generous quantities of wine and beer, racy conversation with his pals and the sight of a pretty girl to poring over theory manuals. It was this roguish facet of his personality that would enable him to empathise so compellingly with the characters in his operas.

Bazzini had been appointed Director at the Conservatoire for the 1881–2 educational year so Puccini was obliged to change his composition tutor to Ponchielli, a younger man with a more easy-going personality. The two hit it off from the start. Additionally, Puccini gained himself a new flatmate: none other than the rising young musical star Pietro Mascagni, who unlike Puccini had clawed himself up the hard way. Indeed, Mascagni would never have become a composer if his baker father had succeeded in grooming his son for the family business. To avoid spending his life working the ovens, in 1876 Mascagni had moved in with his uncle, who had actively supported his musical studies. Such was Mascagni's exceptional rate of progress that within four years he had produced a symphony, some songs and church music; after winning a contest in 1881 with his cantata *In Filanda* he was admitted to the Milan Conservatoire, aged just eighteen. The academic life never really suited the young renegade, however – two years later Mascagni would leave Milan without graduating.

But during the spring of 1882 the two new friends indulged in playing the life of bohemians, cheerfully avoiding creditors by hiding in wardrobes and under beds. On one occasion Puccini pawned his overcoat simply for escorting to dinner a young girl to whom he had taken a fancy. Mascagni was already on a collision course with the Conservatoire, but Puccini managed to keep his head above water – most notably with a new orchestral piece, the nine-minute *Preludio sinfonico*, first performed by a student ensemble on 15 July. The impact Wagner's music had on Puccini is experienced at a very immediate level, and for the first time Verdi barely gets a look in – although there is still very little that is recognisably by Puccini. If for no other reason, the *Preludio* is invaluable for demonstrating the origin of all those heart-aching melodies that Puccini wrote – not *Aida*, not *La Gioconda*, not *Faust*, but Wagner's *Lohengrin*!

Two further orchestral pieces followed in 1883: a four-minute *Adagietto*, the sighing string suspensions of which are strangely reminiscent of the young Elgar, and a twelve-minute, ternary-form *Capriccio sinfonico* – Puccini's graduation piece, premiered on 14 July. He later recollected that he couldn't get this piece out of his head, composing it 'at home, in the street, in class, at the Osteria Aida... I wrote on odd bits of paper and the margins of newspapers'. The opening section is on the dark side of Wagnerian – discontented, gloomy, slightly threatening. Then, about three-and-a-half minutes in, there is a sudden change of mood and we hear what would later be used as the opening bars of *La Bohème*, not merely in embryo, but polished and enchanting.

It is not just hindsight that makes this moment stand out; there is a swaying contentment and creative exuberance that, for the first time in Puccini's music, makes one sit up and listen absorbedly. The subsequent development of these bars into a waltz-tune is less individual and has no place in the later opera, yet overall the work has a compelling sweep and spontaneity that led the influential local critic Filippo Filippi to enthuse that Puccini possessed a 'distinctive and very rare musical temperament'.

Puccini finished his last year at the Conservatoire with his first songs in nearly ten years. Four are settings of poems by the celebrated journalist and novelist Antonio Ghislanzoni from his collection *Melodie per canto*. (Among Ghislanzoni's many and varied achievements were a staggering eighty-five opera librettos, including those of Verdi's *La forza del destino* and *Aida*.) One of the songs, *Melanconia* ('Nostalgia'), has not survived, but *Salve regina*, for soprano and organ/harmonium accompaniment, possesses a chaste, gentle intensity in the popular manner of Gounod or Massenet and incorporates a little motif that clearly anticipates the famous orchestral Intermezzo from Mascagni's *Cavalleria rusticana*. Puccini adapted it just a few months later for the Part One finale of his opera *Le villi*. *Ad una morta!* ('To a Dead Woman!') also furnished ideas for *Le villi* and *Manon Lescaut*, although its occasionally fierce intensity seems closer in mood to *Tosca*. The most polished of the four, however, is *Storiella d'amore* ('Love Story'), an enchanting setting whose idyllic tone suggests a composer very much at ease with himself and in full command of his material.

One final work of the summer of 1883 effectively rounded out Puccini's student years: a dramatic recitative-and-aria setting of a text by Felice Romani entitled *Mentia l'avviso*. (Romani was the most significant librettist in Italian music between Metastasio and Boito, and furnished texts for Bellini, Donizetti and Rossini.) This is a more formal piece than *Storiella d'amore*, a consolidation of existing techniques rather than an exploration of new avenues of expression, yet it is remarkable for an exhilaration in the sheer power and ecstasy of the human voice.

The twenty-four-year-old composer now stood at a musical crossroads. The question was whether he should develop further his recent orchestral successes or pursue the vocal writing for which he had such an obvious talent. The answer was, of course, both – but at the same time. Puccini could no longer deny his true destiny.

Chapter 2

Failure and Success:
Le villi

> “I arrived at the theatre with just
> 40 centissimi in my pocket.
> That was all I had in the world.”

Failure and Success: *Le villi*

As Puccini neared the end of his final year at the Milan Conservatoire his thoughts turned to his future as a professional musician. The fall-back option was taking up the family post in Lucca as organist and choirmaster at San Martino. This carried with it the advantage of a regular income and considerable status in the surrounding area. Another possibility was a teaching post at his Luccan Alma Mater, the Pacini Institute. Neither filled him with much enthusiasm.

Just as it seemed as though Puccini might resign himself to the inevitable, in April 1883 his attention was drawn to a competition announcement by the music publisher Edoardo Sonzogno, in his new journal *Il teatro illustrato*. A prize of 2,000 lire was offered for a one-act opera by an Italian composer in comic, idyllic or dramatic vein, with the proviso that each entry would be anonymous. Puccini knew that he would be up against composers vastly more experienced than himself, but if the only viable alternative was returning home to Lucca, and a life of cosy parochialism, then he was determined to give it his best shot.

To put Puccini's aspirations at this time in perspective, he was clearly one of Ponchielli's most talented pupils, but not yet a star. The general feeling was that Puccini's work was patchy, and that although he showed much promise, he applied himself only when it suited him. Ponchielli, not unreasonably, considered that for someone intending to make composing his career, Puccini was somewhat uncommitted – being disinclined to put pen to paper unless inspiration really struck. When he graduated in the summer of 1883 it was therefore with a copper medal – a significant achievement, but hardly outstanding for a student of his pronounced gifts.

Whatever reservations Ponchielli may have had about Puccini's working methods, he knew raw talent when he saw it and from then on did all he reasonably could to help Puccini make his way in the musical world. He introduced him to Italy's most prestigious music publisher, Giulio Ricordi, and, more importantly in the short term, made sure that Puccini had a fighting chance in the opera competition by putting him in touch with the established poet, playwright and journalist Ferdinando Fontana, with a view to the latter writing a libretto.

Fontana later recollected that Ponchielli first suggested the collaboration with Puccini in a horse-drawn carriage touring the shores of Lake Como. 'Straight away, while the memory of the *Capriccio sinfonico* was still fresh in my mind,' Fontana enthused, 'I came up with a suitably colourful story for the young composer, and outlined the story of *Le villi*.' Composer and librettist seemed to have got on well enough, and in a letter to Ponchielli, Fontana generously suggested that although his nominal charge for a single act was 300 lire, he would be prepared to accept an advance of 100 and receive the balance only if the opera won the competition. Puccini loved the idea of *Le villi* and wrote to his mother excitedly that it gave him plenty of scope for 'descriptive, symphonic music', which he felt was very much his forte at that time.

The legend of the Villis was first adapted by the German Romantic poet Heinrich Heine. It had then been turned into a full-length scenario by Théophile Gautier for Adolphe Adam's classic ballet score *Giselle* of 1846, which tells the story of a band of jilted maidens (Willis) who punish their faithless lovers by dancing them to death. Fontana, however, chose to base his libretto on the more graphic 1852 adaptation by Alphonse Karr, set in the Black Forest. Karr was a former editor of the French newspaper *Le Figaro*, and his caustic wit had won him a group of devoted admirers. Of his many popular aphorisms, the most famous is 'plus ça change, plus c'est la même chose'.

Fontana, remarkably, had the libretto ready in a fortnight. He was nine years Puccini's senior and a working professional well practised in meeting tight deadlines. Puccini, on the other hand, was used to composing on a long leash, had a tendency to back away if something didn't immediately fire his imagination, and had no previous experience of working on such a scale. No doubt aware of how easily he could be distracted in the bustling streets of Milan, Puccini elected to return home to Lucca to give his first magnum opus his fullest attention. For what was probably the first time in his life, Puccini set to his task with supreme discipline, spending several hours a day working flat out, over nearly four months, in order to meet the 31 December deadline.

Even at this early stage the sense of desperation and futility, to the point of neurosis, that would afflict Puccini throughout his life during the creative phase was already apparent. According to his sister, Ramelde:

> After a little while he was assailed by discouragement, doubt and, at the same time, inertia. However, a guardian angel was watching over his destiny, and that was his Mamma... who devoted all her strength to exhorting him, encouraging him, and acting as a critic of what he was writing. Every piece of work was passed to her to judge and Giacomo accepted her judgement and revised and rewrote...

What anxiety, what effort, what trepidation, how many nights she spent with Giacomo!

Puccini quickly discovered the working method that suited him best. He began by composing the vocal line, noting the implied harmonies as he went along. He then revised and expanded upon this basic outline while working on the orchestration. He was a notoriously slow worker, and although he got the job done in the nick of time, he had to send in his original, barely legible scrawlings, having had no time to arrange for a fair copy of the music to be made.

Following this extraordinary, concerted effort, Puccini had to wait almost as long again for the result. He spent weeks agonising over the possible outcome. Was the opera really as good as he'd imagined? Would his inexperience show? Would the five-strong panel – which included his own teacher Ponchielli – even be able to read it? At last, April arrived and the jury announced its decision. There had been twenty-eight submissions in total, of which only five measured up to the exactingly high standards of the competition – and Puccini's *Le villi* was not among them. It seems that Puccini was neither unduly surprised nor despondent at the news. After all, his musical handwriting would have tried the patience of a saint, and one of the stated conditions of entry was that each score should be 'clearly legible'. Under the circumstances, even Ponchielli wouldn't have been able to save him.

Although Puccini took the news squarely on the jaw, there was still the question of his future to consider. Was he to falter at the first operatic hurdle? Fontana was determined not to be beaten, however, and through a journalist contact he arranged an opportunity for Puccini to play and sing through the score to an influential group that included Catalani (future composer of *La Wally*), music publisher Giulio

Ricordi and Boito. Victory was snatched from the jaws of defeat: the assembled party was unanimous in its praise, and a performance was quickly arranged at the Teatro dal Verme in Milan. It was given on 31 May to rapturous applause. Puccini was called to take a bow no fewer than eighteen times and the press was ecstatic: one journalist excitedly referred to Puccini as 'the next Bizet or Massenet'. In just over a month, mild dejection had turned to elation.

It didn't end there. The curtain had barely come down following the last of four performances of *Le villi* when Ricordi pounced and made Puccini an offer he couldn't refuse. Not only did he purchase the exclusive rights to *Le villi* but he invited Puccini and Fontana to write a follow-up, granting the composer a guaranteed monthly stipend for the next two years in order to free him from any undue financial pressures. Additionally he asked Puccini to restructure *Le villi* in two acts so as to enhance its commercial appeal. The young composer could hardly believe his luck. 'Huge success, all hopes fulfilled,' he excitedly telegraphed his mother.

> *I arrived at the theatre with just 40 centissimi in my pocket. That was all I had in the world. And just one suit – a shambolic, coffee-brown suit in which I had to receive the cheers and applause when I was called out in front of the curtain. But just a few days later Giulio Ricordi bought the rights to my opera and handed me the first thousand lire notes of my life.*

Puccini's achievement was not inconsiderable: Ricordi had under copyright at that time the operas of Rossini, Bellini, Donizetti and Verdi.

Good news travels fast and it was around this time that the seventy-one-year-old Verdi caught wind of the musical storm whipped up by the young man destined to inherit his operatic throne. Within two weeks of *Le villi*'s premiere Verdi had mentioned Puccini in a letter, and although at this point Verdi could not possibly have heard a single note of the score, someone – probably Ricordi – was clearly keeping him well informed.

I have heard some good things about Puccini. He is a modernist by instinct, which is entirely understandable, although his emphasis on melody is neither old-fashioned nor contemporary. However, he does appear to emphasise the symphonic aspect. There's nothing wrong in that except that he will need to tread carefully. Opera is opera and the symphony is the symphony, and it would be a mistake to insert music of a symphonic nature into an operatic score, simply to give the orchestra something to do.

However, Puccini soon suffered a cruel twist of fate almost the equal of anything that occurs in his operas: just as he was riding high on an initial wave of musical and critical success, he had to come to terms with the fact that his mother, aged just fifty-four, was mortally ill. On 17 July she passed away, dealing the young composer a body blow that left him emotionally winded for several months. He said in a letter that any successes the future might bring would feel hollow without his mother by his side. 'I'm a composer,' he wrote, 'but after my mother's death I became a corpse.' One of Puccini's close friends at this time described him as looking 'like a ghost' – the loss of the endlessly supportive and utterly devoted Albina at a time when she would surely have been glowing with pride proved almost unbearable.

Puccini turned to work for solace, burying himself in the revisions to *Le villi*, which kept him fully occupied until the middle of November. He couldn't face the family home and so went to stay with his recently married sister, Ramelde, just a few kilometres outside Lucca. The revisions to the original score were important but not unduly onerous. The two most important additions were Anna's Act I cavatina 'Se come voi piccina io fossi', destined to become the most regularly performed item from the score, and Roberto's Act II scena in which he sings of a strange sense of foreboding as the Willis begin to emerge from the forest.

The premiere of the two-act revision of *Le villi* was given at the Teatro Regio in Turin on 26 December. It was a shambolic affair, featuring a cast of second-rate vocalists under an indifferent conductor. One can sense the helplessness felt by Puccini and Fontana in a jointly signed letter they sent to Ricordi. In it the singers are described as 'over the hill', the chorus as 'pitifully weak', the orchestra as 'incompetent and half-asleep'. They also had the appalling acoustics of the Regio Theatre to contend with and could only wonder at what the scenery might be like as they hadn't even been allowed to see it. 'Puccini is thoroughly pessimistic about it all', Fontana adds. 'However, I believe that despite everything we have a success on our hands.' In the event, *Le villi* was tolerably well received, although Puccini was called on stage for a decidedly moderate four curtain calls.

Neither man was particularly affected by the Turin experience, however, as both were more preoccupied by the work's Milan premiere at La Scala on 24 January 1885. This was a much more professional affair. Franco Faccio, the highly experienced chief conductor at La Scala, had secured an excellent cast, including the soprano Romilda Pantaleoni (who two years later would sing Desdemona in the premiere of Verdi's *Otello*).

The La Scala production of *Le villi* was an event of the greatest significance for both Puccini and Fontana, and it

appears to have been received well enough, securing a run of *La Scala, Milan*
thirteen performances. But although Ricordi's idea of revising
the opera had greatly improved its musical and dramatic
structure, the fact that its two acts only weighed in at just
over an hour was taken as rather short measure by some. And
the main criticism was that in general there was not enough
singing and too much orchestra. The Italians expected a
night out at the opera to be completely dominated by the
performers on stage – the instrumentalists in the pit were a
necessary convenience, but of no real interest in themselves.
How things would change over the next decade! Puccini
added an aria for Roberto at around this time ('Torna ai felici
dì', which still occasionally appears in solo recitals), but left
what some critics described as the 'symphonic' presence of
the orchestra undiminished.

The operatic world, though, was alerted to a major new
presence. And Puccini had achieved this with the odds stacked
against him. Not only was he completely inexperienced as

an opera composer, he had had to turn *Le villi* around in a relatively short space of time, under the kind of work pressure that he had studiously avoided in the past. He had also been saddled with a run-of-the-mill libretto decidedly short on dramatic incident, and drawn from the German tradition of apparitions and mystical beings – hardly a happy hunting-ground for Italian composers; his inexperience had led him to accept Fontana's text word for word, something which he would never dream of doing in years to come. Yet such was his determination to succeed that he overcame all these obstacles and produced a piece of work of which he could feel justly proud.

Puccini's sensitivity to atmosphere and to the magic of being in love is evident from the start and saves from floundering a half-hour first act in which very little happens. The two-and-a-half-minute Prelude is more notable for its gently diverting stream of ideas than for any sense of organic cohesion. Yet it demonstrates a keen awareness of Wagnerian (and recent Verdian) trends towards integrating the prelude into the first act proper, and is a succinct introduction to a number of ideas that will be heard later in the opera. If the opening double pedal-point is not a device one especially associates with Puccini, the gently sighing violin writing with its heaving downward intervals (especially the falling 5th) and the chains of gentle harmonic suspensions provide a stylistic blueprint for his later work.

At six minutes in length (roughly a quarter of the first act) the opening scene of villagers celebrating Anna and Roberto's engagement is a shade indulgent, but it at least gives the opportunity to hear some uncharacteristically Sullivanesque high spirits in the opening F major section, and a touch of bohemian rusticity when the music draws on the A minor Scherzo for string quartet, now scored for orchestra.

Le villi

Act I: As the curtain rises, Anna, the daughter of Guglielmo the woodsman, announces her engagement to her beloved Roberto, much to the approval of the other villagers. However, it transpires that Roberto must leave immediately for Mainz in order to claim an inheritance left to him by a deceased aunt. Anna is disturbed at the prospect of being separated from Roberto so soon, especially as she has been troubled by dark premonitions. Roberto makes light of her worries, insisting that he will remain faithful to her come what may.

Act II: By the time he arrives in Mainz, however, Anna is but a dim and distant memory. He soon finds himself luxuriating in the arms of a beautiful courtesan, and, seduced by the riches of the big city, resolves never to return to his village. Anna, meanwhile, becomes increasingly distraught at Roberto's absence before collapsing and dying of a broken heart in the winter frosts.

Overcome with grief, Anna's father summons the Willis, spirits of jilted virgins who live in the dark forest. Desperate and dishevelled, he asks them to take Anna's soul and avenge her death. On reflection he regrets his hastiness in summoning the spirits and begs God for his forgiveness. Meanwhile Roberto, now penniless and rejected by his lover, has seen the error of his ways and returns to the village to try to put things right. On the edge of the forest he is met by Anna's ghost, who tells him that his callous behaviour hurt her so much that she couldn't bear to go on living. Roberto breaks down and repents, but it is too late. Bent on revenge, the Willis encircle him and Anna's ghost hurtles Roberto into a frenzied dance of death.

With Anna's aria 'Se come voi piccina io fossì, o vaghi fior' ('If I were like you, pretty flowers'), Puccini is in more familiar territory and produces a touching melody which could be the work of no one else. The harmony is more succulent than before, there are *Bohème*-like moments when the clarinet doubles the rising vocal line, and Puccini delays and then times the climax to perfection. Nevertheless, he does not yet build up the emotional heads of steam familiar from the mature operas; although the melody is beautifully crafted and developed, it ultimately lacks the memorability and distinction of those given to later heroines.

The most inimitable passage of this section occurs when Roberto requests a smile; the music suggests the quiet intimacy and glow of this special moment with so great a precision that it feels as though one could reach out and touch it. Nothing much is happening, yet such is the emotional sincerity of Puccini's writing that it doesn't seem to matter. On hearing this one can well understand why some early observers felt that Verdi's natural successor had already arrived.

Having flexed his creative muscles for Anna, Puccini now produces a virtual prototype for his later tenor principals Rodolfo, Cavaradossi and Pinkerton in Roberto's aria 'Mio cherubino, perchè' ('From the days of my childhood'). Even at this early stage Puccini demonstrates an ability to turn operatic rhetoric on its head. Where most composers would invariably introduce the main male character in an imposing fashion, Puccini steals in, allowing the music, through the repetition of short phrases, to gain gradually in intensity. He subtly amplifies the domestic emotions of kitchen-sink drama for the opera house, rather than imbuing his characters with a heroic stance that sits uncomfortably with their station in life.

Although totally at home in the love music, Puccini seems to lose his individual voice at the start of the following scene when the lovers say their farewells. One can almost sense him creatively thinking out loud as he grafts an unmistakably Verdian melody onto liquid phrases more reminiscent of Wagner. We are at least treated to the first of Puccini's supercharged climaxes that would find their apex in Musetta's waltz song from Act II of *La Bohème*.

Roberto's heady indulgences in Mainz are not shown, but briefly described by a Narrator to the accompaniment of a dreamy five-minute musical Interlude, following which the Narrator then outlines the legend of the Willis and Roberto's return to the homeland. The music which introduces the second act proper is dramatically imposing and in contrast to anything heard up to that point (the so-called 'Witches' Dance'). Tellingly, it is a skipping figure dancing over a simple added-note chord that truly arrests the attention, rather than the Verdian angst which dominates the section as a whole. Guglielmo's recitative and aria is intensely melodramatic, and even Roberto's extended 'Torna ai felici dì' is a variety of solo set-piece that Puccini would mostly avoid later. This was Puccini heading close to the *verismo* style which was then all the rage – the emotional power is indisputable, but a reliance on generic hysteria à la Mascagni cannot be denied.

With the appearance of the Willis comes the only dramatic action of the entire opera. The situation is straight out of the mystical tradition begun with Weber's *Der Freischütz* and continued by Wagner in *Der fliegende Holländer*, although Puccini has two further aces up his sleeve: Anna's touching recollections of Roberto's words from the opening act, which build wave upon wave towards exultant climaxes, and then the closing bars which drive Roberto's punishment home in pulverising fashion.

If *Le villi* remains an uneven work constrained by a less than inspired libretto, it is ultimately saved by Puccini's invention. Until this point there had been only tantalising glimpses of Puccini's capabilities, but *Le villi* provided the most consistent evidence yet of his extraordinary talent. The opera is in many ways the key that unlocks the door of his later music.

Chapter 3

Elvira and *Edgar*

Elvira and *Edgar*

The success of *Le villi* left Ricordi in no doubt that a follow-up was in order – and as soon as possible. Puccini was on something of an artistic high, but his day-to-day life had become more complicated following the death of his mother. Fortunately his five sisters – Iginia, Nitteti, Otilia, Ramelde and Tomaide – had all left home, leaving just his younger brother, Michele. With some string-pulling from Puccini and his former teacher Bazzini, Michele gained a place at the Milan Conservatoire; but after three years of decidedly average progress he was to opt out and head instead for South America.

Another distraction for Puccini from writing a new opera was his adulterous affair with Elvira Gemignani, the wife of a successful Luccan merchant, Narciso, a former school-friend of Puccini's. Although it is difficult to place a reliable date on Puccini's and Elvira's first encounter, it seems that the two were at least aware of each other by the time of *Le villi*'s La Scala premiere in January 1885.

Elvira's husband was often away on business trips during which he would play away from home as much as many Italian men of the period. Elvira's and Puccini's relationship therefore had the conditions necessary to flourish; the couple's attempts at subterfuge were abandoned and they began appearing openly in public together. Inevitably, the affair set tongues wagging, although Narciso appears to have been kept in the dark as to the precise nature of his wife's relationship.

Sometime during the spring of 1886 Elvira fell pregnant with Puccini's child, and by the autumn concealment was no longer an option. It seems that, even at this late stage, Narciso had assumed that the baby was his, although that came to an abrupt end when he returned one evening to discover the house in turmoil and to be told that his wife had deserted him for Puccini, taking their daughter Fosca with her. Elvira tried to throw her family off the scent by informing them she was heading for Palermo. In reality she was hiding at secret addresses in the surrounding area. Meanwhile both she and Puccini were ostracised not only by their respective families but by the local community, which was buzzing with the sensational news. Not until Narciso's death in 1903 would Elvira finally be free to marry Puccini.

Elvira, Puccini's future wife, c. 1900

In December 1886 Elvira gave birth to a son, Antonio, which put even greater strain on Puccini's already dwindling finances. As a result the couple and their new charge spent most of the next five years flitting from one location to another, at one point even living apart in order to save money by staying with friends (while misinforming them that they had split up). Ricordi had meanwhile agreed to an extension of Puccini's basic allowance beyond the initial year while working on the new opera.

Puccini was every bit as devoted to Elvira as she was to him, yet apart from the strong physical attraction theirs was hardly a match made in heaven. Puccini was simply not born to be monogamous, and Elvira was the jealous type, deeply suspicious of any female he came into contact with. Puccini enjoyed the great outside, revelling in fast cars and boats, and the gentlemanly pursuits of hunting and fishing – none of which held any appeal for Elvira. Most crucially, she had no interest in 'serious' music, or indeed the arts in general. From the start, there was an aesthetic chasm between the pair. As time went by, they found it increasingly difficult to spend long periods of time together. Yet, like opposing poles on a magnet, there was between them an irresistible attraction which, even when placed under severe pressure, prevented them from separating permanently.

Given Puccini's churning emotions at this time, his severe lack of funds, his elopement with Elvira, the constant changes of address, his virtual banishment from Lucca and his unplanned entry into fatherhood, it is a miracle that he found time to concentrate on anything else, let alone a full-scale opera in three acts. That the task took him so long to complete (three years for the first version) is perhaps less than surprising under the circumstances. Yet the hiatuses in his personal life were mere drops in the ocean compared to the almost insurmountable problem that Fontana had presented

him with: a libretto that was truly awful, entitled *Edgar*.

Fontana was instinctively drawn to literature rather than to the theatre. Considering his inexperience as a librettist and the problems with inactivity and dramatic thrust that are only too clear in *Le villi*, one might have expected him to play safe with a tried and tested drama. In the event he chose a play in verse (or 'poème dramatique') by one of his favourite writers, Alfred de Musset (1810–1857): *La*

Coupe et les lèvres ('The Cup and the Lips'). This was never originally intended for stage presentation, and when Musset had first tried it out on members of his literary circle their general reaction was so indifferent that the piece was swiftly consigned to the bottom drawer. Yet, incredibly, this is the very work that Fontana decided was right for Puccini, and the composer accepted it calmly.

The first draft of the libretto was ready for Puccini to start composing in May 1885, just four months after *Le villi*'s La Scala premiere. Whatever the suitability of Fontana's choice of text and workability of his adaptation, no one could accuse him of dalliance. As for Puccini, work was slow from the start. It was originally anticipated that *Edgar* would be ready within the year, but with the Elvira affair in full swing, sapping his energies, the work proceeded in fits and starts. It was not until September 1888 that the ink was dry on the final page.

It would be wrong to assume that the three years it took to compose the first version of *Edgar* (in four acts) were totally dominated by domestic upheaval. Throughout this period Puccini continued to attend performances not only of *Le villi* but such recent landmark works as Verdi's *Falstaff* (in Trieste) and Wagner's *Parsifal* – Puccini and the ever-devoted Fontana made the pilgrimage to Bayreuth to hear the opera at the 1888 Festival. Indeed, Fontana was a constant source of both personal and financial support for the composer, even though he himself had taken up with a married woman who strongly disapproved of both Puccini and Elvira.

Around this time, Puccini composed the short song *Sole e amore* for a Genoese periodical. Surprisingly, this turned out to be the most indelible melody he had produced since the orchestral *Capriccio sinfonico* of 1883. Like the *Capriccio*, *Sole e amore* would later furnish material for *La Bohème*, in this case the end of Act III.

However, uppermost in Puccini's mind was the forthcoming La Scala premiere of *Edgar* on 21 April 1889. Rehearsals proved something of a trial due to the occasionally challenging nature of the music – Puccini's compositional techniques and harmonic vocabulary were continuing to develop, including his use of dissonance. But conductor Franco Faccio, who had been on the podium for the premiere of Verdi's *Otello* two years earlier, ensured that all ran smoothly on the night. The singers once again included Romilda Pantaleoni, and Ricordi promoted the event assiduously. All was set for a memorable evening, and everyone involved hoped to see the thirty-year-old Puccini confirmed as Italy's leading light among its younger musicians. In fact, the only person to sound a note of caution was Puccini himself.

In the event, Puccini's apprehension proved justified, even if the premiere wasn't the unmitigated disaster that some sources suggest. The most level-headed review, in the influential *Corriere della sera* newspaper, praised certain passages while pointing out that others, although perfectly effective, were somewhat reminiscent of Bizet and Gounod. The same report revealed that Puccini was called out for applause on three occasions during the second act. Yet bearing in mind the high expectations the event had excited, both press and audience appear, in the main, to have been decidedly underwhelmed. After just three performances *Edgar* was dropped from the schedule.

The ever-resourceful Ricordi immediately embarked on an exercise in damage limitation. At first the publisher's financial backers wanted Puccini removed from the composer roster; they were quickly silenced when Ricordi himself threatened to leave if his young protégé was shown the door. He also guaranteed to offset out of his own pocket any short-term costs involved in keeping Puccini under exclusive contract.

In a letter to the beleaguered young composer, Ricordi makes his devoted support unequivocal:

> *Remember that you are in one of the most critical and difficult moments of your artistic life. I say this not because of the idiocies poured forth by our famous music critics, but because now we must open a breach, scale it with courage and perseverance, and there plant a victorious flag... I read in* Edgar *clearly all your gifts, all the hopes of the future. But to realise these hopes it is necessary to follow one motto: Excelsior!*

Following long discussions with both composer and librettist, substantial revisions and cuts were made over the summer during a stay at Lake Como. This second version, premiered at Lucca's Teatro del Giglio, still left much to be desired: for in discarding material which held up the action, Puccini undermined the characterisations. The ill-fated *Edgar* would go on to become the most-revised of all Puccini's operas.

Even with Ricordi to help prop him up, Puccini was becoming increasingly despondent about all aspects of his life. In a letter to his brother Michele dated 24 April 1890, he moaned that he was about to be kicked out of his Milan digs 'for playing the piano at night' and that he was 'sick of the eternal struggle with poverty'. One event cheered him enormously, however:

> *Buffalo Bill has been here. I enjoyed the show. They are a company of North Americans with some Red Indians and buffaloes. They perform magnificent feats of shooting and give realistic presentations of scenes that have happened on the frontier. In eleven days they drew 120,000 lire!*

While engaged in further substantial revisions to *Edgar* in the spring of 1891, Puccini was devastated to read the news that Michele, who had gone to work in South America, had died. At first all had seemed well for him there – Michele had secured a job as a music teacher and, like his older brother, relished the many opportunities for outdoor pursuits, especially hunting. Unfortunately, he also shared with Giacomo an eye for the ladies and soon found himself embroiled in an affair with a married woman of some distinction. A duel ensued, following which Michele was obliged to leave the remote Andean town that had become his base; he eventually ended up in Rio de Janeiro, where he succumbed to yellow fever, aged only twenty-seven. Puccini and his sisters were grief-stricken.

Work on *Edgar* eventually culminated in a much-curtailed third version, now in three acts. It was given on 28 February 1892 in Ferrara under Puccini's stage direction. If hardly a runaway success, it was sufficiently well received for Puccini's spirits to be raised and for a Madrid performance to be planned for 19 March. With Ricordi's help he even managed to persuade the great tenor and Verdi's original Otello, Francesco Tamagno, to sing the lead role. Additionally he added a gently swaying, Hispanically flavoured Prelude to Act I. With the Queen of Spain in attendance it proved to be something of a gala occasion. Yet although four numbers were encored and the Queen personally invited Puccini up to her box to offer him her congratulations, the six-performance run was, by the standards of Puccini's later operas, a moderate success at best.

A lesser composer might have left it that, but Puccini was still determined to try to knock *Edgar* into some kind of satisfactory shape. For a while he seriously considered reinstating the fourth act and dumping the second with which he had grown increasingly dissatisfied. Some idea of the extent of the cuts can be gleaned from the fact that the 1890 version contained twenty-seven scenes, and the 1892 version eighteen. More than a decade later, in 1905, and with four successful operas under his belt, Puccini again decided to tighten the structure of *Edgar* in a few places in order to produce a 'definitive' version; this was unveiled in Buenos Aires on 8 July, although Puccini still wasn't satisfied. Ultimately, he seems to have washed his hands of the work that proved to be his one real failure, referring to it as 'una cantonata' – a blunder. The original vocal score – liberally coated by Puccini with such disparaging remarks as 'May God protect you from this opera' and 'the most horrible thing ever written' – says it all. At least Puccini managed to salvage some of the music and adapt it for *Tosca*.

For audiences still dazzled by Verdi's *Otello*, *Edgar*'s dramatic shortcomings would have seemed all too obvious. It shares with *Otello* a plot revolving around the murderous power of anger, fuelled by jealousy. In Verdi's (and Shakespeare's) scenario the action is confined essentially to three characters in a single, specific location; by contrast, Fontana's plot – involving changes of location, public confrontations and disguises – is confusing. And musically, Puccini's dilutions of the Italian style with 'foreign' importations – Massenet, Meyerbeer and Bizet most especially – would hardly have met with general approval on home soil. Wagner's influence is evident less in the music itself (although it occasionally emerges out of the rolling textures) than in the way that the various elements mesh together in one continuous sweep, bound by musical cross-referencing. This means the appearance of motifs, or 'tags', introduced by the orchestra, which are associated with various characters (though not, in this case, Edgar himself). Where Puccini's motifs differ from Wagner's is that they remain relatively

Edgar

Act I: The scene is a village in Flanders, in 1302. Edgar is fast asleep in front of a village inn. First on the scene is Fidelia, who is infatuated with the young man and playfully breaks a twig off a tree, presenting it to him. Coyly she rushes off, but before Edgar can give chase he is accosted by Tigrana, his former lover who is insanely jealous of Fidelia. She taunts him with reminders of former times, the memories of which incense Edgar who scuttles off angrily back home. Next appears Fidelia's brother Frank, who is besotted with Tigrana; she, it transpires, was abandoned by a Moorish army in childhood and grew up with Fidelia and Frank in their family home. Tigrana makes her lack of interest in Frank painfully clear and leaves him to ponder his churning emotions.

In a scene straight out of Bizet's *Carmen*, Tigrana nails her colours firmly to the mast with a shameless display of earthy sensuality in which she attempts to drown out the congregation's singing in the nearby church with a decidedly secular verse of her own, before being driven straight into the arms of Edgar, who has come to see what all the fuss is about. With a rush of blood to the head, Edgar curses the villagers, sets fire to his house, injures Frank in a fight and escapes with Tigrana, vowing to lead a life of opulent indulgence from then on.

Act II: In luxurious surroundings (no exact location is given), a chorus is extolling the pleasures of life. Edgar emerges looking gloomy and dejected. He castigates himself for having ever left the village and the arms of his innocent beloved, Fidelia. When Tigrana attempts to lift him out of his reverie he admonishes her as a 'demon' and clearly wants no more to do with her. A platoon of soldiers happens by, whose captain turns out to be none other than Frank. Soon all differences are forgotten – Frank has even forgiven Edgar for wounding him in their fight, for it finally brought him to his senses regarding Tigrana. The two friends head off arm-in-arm, leaving Tigrana to plan her revenge.

Act III: A military funeral procession files past following the body of a fallen comrade in full armour; it appears Frank is among the followers next to a monk whose face is obscured by a hood. Behind them are Fidelia and her father Gualtiero. The 'dead' soldier's identity becomes clear as Fidelia cries out in anguish for 'Edgar, Edgar, my only love'. The hooded monk now moves slowly among the crowd explaining that with his dying breath Edgar had wanted his sins to be publicly aired by way of penance. As the monk rehearses Edgar's list of misdemeanours the crowd becomes increasingly restless, and when it begins to move menacingly towards the knight's body, Fidelia dispels the situation by pleading for mercy.

Tigrana now appears on the scene; Frank and the monk goad her into speaking out against Edgar. With the promise of jewellery as a reward she obliges. Once again the masses become indignant and surge towards the armoured hero only to find that there isn't a body. Edgar throws off his monkish disguise and reveals he is very much alive! Cursing Tigrana he throws his arms around Fidelia in a moment of transfiguration. This is all too much for the vengeful Tigrana who flings herself on Fidelia, stabbing her straight through the heart. As the crowd stands numb with shock at what has happened, soldiers lead Tigrana away to her death.

unchanged at every appearance, rather than being used for symphonic or dramatic development.

The opening scene is enchanting, its piquant woodwind and cascading strings effectively counterpointed by harp and glockenspiel. Pentatonic (five-note) melodic shapes combine with a sense of open-air freshness that looks forward to *Madama Butterfly*. Puccini's favourite compound, skipping rhythms gently cajole events along, while his delight in musical opposites being brought into close proximity can be savoured at the moment of the temptress Tigrana's first entry: this blazes forth in the orchestra (Tigrana's motto is spat out with strangulated fury by the brass) and then continues with music of the utmost delicacy.

If considered purely as a flow of musical ideas, the advances on *Le villi* are thus far unmistakable: there is a much greater sense of creative individuality and confidence, with less reliance on recitative to cover the dramatic joins. It is when one takes a closer look at what is being sung that a certain unevenness becomes noticeable. Puccini was already adept at conveying emotional extremes (uncontainable joy and exuberance, heart-fluttering naivety, insidious evil); yet when Tigrana reflects upon the passion that she and Edgar once shared, the emotional temperature is at a curiously moderate setting, as if Puccini is uncertain how to pitch it (perhaps because he shamelessly borrows music from the Kyrie belonging to his *Messa a quattro voci* of 1880). When Frank sings of his love for Tigrana, Puccini raises the expressive stakes considerably, which has the effect of making Frank's feelings seem more central to the drama than anyone else's. It's a precursor to Puccini's many soaring solo melodies, and one can't help but feel that it should have gone to the title role — especially as the opening act is past its halfway point.

The uncertain dramatic focus is further exacerbated by the return of the colourful Tigrana. Her altercations with the assembled peasants climax in an unashamedly Verdian march and an outburst from the brass section of high-speed, chromatic heroics that are straight out of the Sanctus from the older composer's Requiem. Edgar's reappearance at this point pushes the action on to the end of the act; yet just as the drama is being propelled forwards, Puccini's independent, creative voice begins to falter in a series of Weberesque tremolandos then a forceful finish of both middle-period Verdian heroics and a grand opulence that recalls Ponchielli. Strangely, the further one travels into this act, especially from around halfway through, the less one senses Puccini's hand on the musical rudder.

At just fifteen minutes, the second act is the shortest of the three. The jaunty, energetic orchestral opening contrasts effectively with the distant meditations of an off-stage chorus extolling the pleasures of life. There follows a winding, melancholy clarinet melody that Puccini surely recalled when composing the famous tenor aria 'E lucevan le stelle' for Act III of *Tosca*. Edgar's opening recitative, in which he complains of growing weary of sensual indulgence, is pointedly accompanied by the most intense piece of Wagnerian chromaticism in the entire work. The unveiling of Wagner's *Tristan und Isolde* in 1868 had revolutionised thinking about key structures in music: characters' innermost feelings, while articulated partially in words, were now being delivered by the orchestra, and this presupposed an endlessly fluid approach to melody and harmony. Though Puccini was rarely slavishly Wagnerian, he was not immune to the German's new thinking, which had an impact on the formation of his style. Here, though, his masterstroke is the way he infuses the music with a warm glow at the words 'Souvra un sereno' ('The sweetest of pictures') as Edgar recalls his beloved angel, Fidelia. A Tchaikovskyan instinct for melodic climax here radiates outwards with an expressive power that would not sound out of place in the pages of Puccini's final opera *Turandot*.

In Tigrana's duet with Edgar that follows, Puccini again appears to hold back from portraying her as a manipulative schemer. Indeed, as the pair go soaring aloft one might readily assume that they were closely bonded rather than drifting irrevocably apart. The reason for this is simple: the music was rescued from the abandoned fourth act where it would originally have been sung by Fidelia! The sound of the approaching marching army is pure *Carmen*, but the biggest surprise is the proud, Elgar-like tread of the music that follows when Frank emerges on the scene. Although Puccini's assessment of the final section as 'the most horrible thing that has ever been written' seems unduly harsh, the second act is particularly uneven.

Toscanini thought so much of the enchanting Prelude to Act III that he conducted it at Puccini's funeral in 1924. The ensuing scene (in which Puccini makes great use of his *Capriccio sinfonico*) marshals the assembled choral forces – boys, proletarians, soldiers, monks – to stirring effect, although with nothing like the virtuoso bravado of *La Bohème*'s second act. One particularly nice touch is the way in which Fidelia's Act I music is recalled as she bids her final farewell to the coffin. As the atmosphere becomes gradually more threatening, the music reverts to the impersonal generic effects of the first act – it is almost as though Puccini is experiencing a crisis of artistic identity as the drama unfolds. Fidelia's arresting 'Nel villaggio d'Edgar' ('I too was born in Edgar's village') is altogether more convincing, and one of the few passages considered by Puccini to be worth preserving.

CD 1 [7]

From here to the end, flashes of inspiration come and go as tantalising hints of Puccini's later work filter in and out of the textures. Yet despite some striking moments, stylistically the final act fails to gel. Puccini was particularly suited to expanding action from a domestic scale to an operatic level, whereas with the final act of *Edgar* he was presented with a story that was already epic in its design. So here he fell back on stock-in-trade devices that complement rather than transform and elevate the action.

Arguments have long raged as to whether *Le villi* or *Edgar* is the finer work. *Le villi* is without doubt the more satisfying dramatic and stylistic unit. It rarely aspires to what it can't deliver, and it largely feels comfortable in its own creative skin. The best sections of *Edgar* leave *Le villi* in the starting-blocks; and yet as a dramatic and stylistic whole it lurches so unpredictably and at times inorganically that it barely sounds like the work of the same composer. *Edgar* begins with some of the most inspired, sincere and warm-hearted music that Puccini had produced up till that point, and ends in the cold, impersonal world of clichéd melodrama.

Composers are not necessarily their own best critics, but Puccini's dissatisfaction with *Edgar* was not terribly wide of the mark. The question that remained was whether Ricordi would lose faith over *Edgar*, or whether he felt it was worth giving the protégé on whom he had invested so much time, energy and money a chance to redeem himself and fulfil his true potential.

Chapter 4

Recovery Vehicle:
Manon Lescaut

Manon is the work of a genius
conscious of his own power,
master of his art, a creator
and perfector of it...

Recovery Vehicle: *Manon Lescaut*

Despite Puccini's best efforts *Edgar* had proved an honourable failure – undeniably full of promise, with flashes of scorching inspiration along the way, yet dramatically and musically uneven. Whenever the characters in *Edgar* turned poetically introspective Puccini was in his element, but crowd scenes and spiritual symbolism did not play to his strengths – it was the raw emotion of the individual that invariably sparked his creativity. The time was fast approaching when he and his librettist would have to part company.

To make things worse, Puccini's former room-mate at the Milan Conservatory, Pietro Mascagni, leapt to international stardom just as Puccini's creative flame showed signs of dimming. The spectacle-hungry Italian audiences of the time wanted searing, unadulterated melodrama – and for a while Mascagni seemed the right man to give it to them. After leaving the Milan Conservatory without graduating, Mascagni had gone on tour with a travelling opera company and then settled in the small town of Cerignola, where he taught music. That might have been the end of his composing aspirations if it hadn't been for the devoted support of his wife Lina, who encouraged him to try the same prestigious Sonzogno competition that Puccini had entered in its inaugural year with *Le villi*. It looked as though Mascagni was going to send in the final act of his recently completed *Guglielmo Ratcliff*,

FRANCHETTI   MASCAGNI   PUCCINI

but Lina interceded and secretly posted off his one-act opera *Cavalleria rusticana* instead. The rest is history. Premiered on 17 May 1890, it created such a furore that it received no fewer than thirty curtain calls (sixty if you believe Mascagni's personal recollection). Within two years *Cavalleria rusticana* had been heard in virtually every major centre throughout the musical world. The speed of its success was unprecedented, while its gritty realism and dramatic concision became the model for *verismo*.

Puccini, Mascagni and Alberto Franchetti

All this was in the near future when Ricordi in the summer of 1889 gave Puccini the green light to start work on a third opera. Having rejected a Russian scenario drawn up by the playwright Giuseppe Giacosa, Puccini briefly considered an opera based on Victorien Sardou's *La Tosca*, suggested to him by Fontana. However, during a tour which took in the recently opened Eiffel Tower and productions of Wagner's *Die Meistersinger* and *Parsifal* at Bayreuth, Puccini settled on the Abbé Prévost's novel *L'Histoire du Chevalier des Grieux et de Manon Lescaut.* Some critics ungenerously noted that the storyline about a woman destroyed by her desire for love and money had been adapted many times before, most notably by Jules Massenet (*Manon*, 1884). But Puccini would have none of it. 'A woman like Manon,' he dryly pointed out, 'can accommodate more than one lover!' He also announced prior to starting work that 'Massenet feels it as a Frenchman, with the powder and the minuets. I shall feel it as an Italian, with desperate passion.'

Having informed a crestfallen Fontana that, despite having come up with the idea of *Manon Lescaut*, his services as librettist were no longer required, Puccini at first considered making the adaptation himself. He quickly saw sense, however, and following Ricordi's advice sought out someone with operatic experience; the first name out of the hat was Ruggero Leoncavallo, who was just a year older than the composer. Puccini knew that his reputation was on the line and that he simply couldn't risk another *Edgar*. This made him particularly edgy during *Manon Lescaut*'s gestation period: Leoncavallo found himself unwittingly in the firing line and quickly taken off the project. But that wasn't the end of the story. As Leoncavallo later put it, 'I shut myself up in my house, and in five months I wrote the poem and music of *Pagliacci*.' From the ashes of *Manon Lescaut* Leoncavallo went on to produce the greatest single success of his career.

Every visitor to Bayreuth seems to come away profoundly affected, and Puccini's experience of the Wagner festival resulted in the most blatantly Wagnerian of his compositions: a seven-minute elegy for string quartet entitled *Crisantemi* (1890). Occasioned by the death of Amadeo, Duke of Aosta, a member of the Italian royal family, it was composed in a single night. The title reflects the chrysanthemum's symbolic connection with funerals and imposing state occasions in Italy. The work's chromatic indulgences pay homage to *Tristan und Isolde*, and although one would be hard-pressed to guess its composer there is undeniably a new expressive confidence in Puccini's writing. Not particularly gratefully written and somewhat over-ripe for pure chamber music, this poignant miniature nevertheless makes a strong impression. Much of the piece would be reused in *Manon Lescaut*.

Puccini's powers of self-belief were showing little sign of waning, yet he now had other problems to contend with. His relationship with Elvira was still causing consternation among members of both families. Even the devoted Ramelde was forced to put her reputation before loyalty to her brother when he asked her to look after his illegitimate son, Tonio. Puccini was exasperated:

> *You always judge people from gossip... and without looking at the circumstances of the facts. Enough of that! It is urgent to settle this matter in the best way possible, without violence and without any extra shocks... I am telling you that I've decided to make a new life.*

There were also times when Puccini and Elvira were obliged to live apart. During one brief period of separation another of Puccini's sisters put the cat among the pigeons by telling Elvira that Giacomo was involved with someone else and poised to end their relationship. Despite Puccini's utter devotion to her at that time, Elvira never came to terms with the feelings of rage and jealousy that began consuming her. In later life she would secretly follow her husband around (sometimes in disguise) just to make sure that he was behaving himself; she even went so far as to pour bromide into the pockets of Puccini's trousers in the hope of chemically restraining his insatiable libido.

Worst of all for Puccini was the continuing nightmare of the libretto for *Manon Lescaut*. After Leoncavallo, he now turned to the dramatist Marco Praga, who agreed to work on the plot with the help of the poet Domenico Oliva in fashioning the actual words. Within days Praga had the opera mapped out in four acts and won the enthusiastic approval of both Ricordi and Puccini. Oliva quickly set to work on fleshing out the story and Paolo Tosti, celebrated composer of *Serenata* and *Addio*, declared it the most beautiful and effective libretto he had ever encountered. As Praga memorably put it, 'it was the *opéra comique* of which Puccini had always dreamed.'

Things could hardly have gone better – or so it seemed. However, the more Puccini wrestled with the overall concept, the more he found himself moving away from *comique* towards *tragique*. As a result he decided to ditch the entire second act and move the remaining two forward; Praga was asked to devise a new storyline for the final act (as well as make innumerable other alterations). Praga felt that the impact of these changes on the original layout was so devastating that he could no longer continue. This left Oliva to struggle on bravely, implementing Puccini's every whim and fancy with great patience.

The basic problem was that Puccini was effectively learning on the job, feeling his way towards the kind of operatic structure and content that aligned itself as closely as possible with his creative gifts. In discovering himself as a composer he was beginning to crystallise in his own mind the kind of music he was born to write. What he was striving for was the kind of symbiosis achieved by Wagner in his later operas – a divine fusion of music, words and stagecraft so indissoluble that the listener cannot imagine one without the other. For

Oliva this was all very well, but to be on the receiving end of a constantly fluctuating series of additions, excisions and refinements eventually proved too much for the poet and he too exasperatedly withdrew from the project.

Ricordi remained supportive and suggested consulting Giacosa, whose initial idea for Puccini's third opera had been rejected. Giacosa, who understandably didn't want to get embroiled in a work that had already caused so many problems, suggested collaborating with the up-and-coming playwright Luigi Illica. Illica's first job, however, was to dissuade Puccini from pulling out of the project to start work on *Tosca* instead·

> *I went to Ricordi and told him that I thought the subject of* Manon, *which I liked, was altogether more suited to Puccini's temperament. After much toing and froing I managed to win the argument. Puccini gave in on one condition that I should re-do the* Manon *libretto because, as it stood,* it just didn't work.

Puccini kept his focus throughout this harrowing period and with Elvira's agreement began searching for somewhere to live on his own for six months, away from all domestic cares, so that he could begin serious work on *Manon Lescaut*. He found the perfect place in Torre del Lago, a small hamlet in the Luccan province which he had initially discovered as an area of solace following the death of his mother. It was cheap, it could only be reached via a dirt track, the forest, lake and mountain scenery was breathtaking, passing tourists had yet to discover its charms, and the villagers, although somewhat insular, were both friendly and considerate. Like many creative people, Puccini was unpredictable in his mood – boyishly playful one day, deeply melancholic the

Puccini at Torre del Lago

next – but once the locals were used to him he was made extremely welcome.

By the autumn of 1892 even Ricordi's patience was beginning to wear a little thin, so when in September he heard that the end was in sight he was much relieved. A month later the opera which had taken three years to complete, and undergone more intensive and wide-ranging revisions than almost any other in history, was finally ready.

Cast in four acts and described as a 'dramma lirico', the finally approved adaptation of François-Antoine Prévost's *Manon Lescaut* was as dramatically fine-tuned as anything Puccini would produce in later years. Yet he was never completely satisfied with it, most particularly the final act. No fewer than six different versions would be authorised by Puccini, though in later life he was to claim that '*Manon Lescaut* was the only one of my operas that I never really had to worry about'!

The problem as to where *Manon Lescaut* should be first performed was settled fairly easily. To fail at La Scala might do irreparable damage to Puccini's reputation, and in any case Verdi's *Falstaff* was due to be premiered there on 9 February 1893. Ricordi opted for the Teatro Regio in Turin, which had the added advantage of being one of the few places where *Edgar* had gone down reasonably well. The date was set for 1 February, a full week before Milan would be putting up Verdi's name in lights.

In the event, Puccini needn't have worried. Despite his complaining to Elvira during January that none of the voices could be heard properly in rehearsals, the premiere was one of the single greatest triumphs of his career and established his reputation once and for all. Barely twenty minutes into the first act, following the tenor aria 'Tra voi, belle' ('Among you, fair beauties'), Puccini was called up on stage to receive the kind of applause composers may fantasise about but rarely achieve. And so it continued. By the end of the evening composer and cast had received over thirty curtain calls.

The press was ecstatic, one commentator referring to the performance as a seminal moment in Italian history. Giovanni Pozza enthused in *Corriere della sera*:

> Between Edgar *and this* Manon, *Puccini has vaulted an abyss.* Edgar *can be said to have been a necessary preparation;* Manon *is the work of a genius conscious of his own power, master of his art, a creator and perfector of it... Puccini's genius is truly Italian. His song is the song of our ancestors... It caresses us and becomes part of us.*

Within the year *Manon* had been produced in South America, Russia, Spain and Germany – the last of these a performance in Hamburg conducted by no less a figure than Gustav Mahler. Although Mahler later developed a strong dislike of Puccini's music he was initially a great admirer, and he had conducted the German premiere of *Le villi*, also in Hamburg.

Something of the flavour of *Manon Lescaut*'s extraordinary impact on the operatic world at large can be gathered from a perspicacious review by George Bernard Shaw following the work's Covent Garden premiere in 1894:

> *There is a genuine symphonic modification, development, and occasionally combination of the thematic material, all in a dramatic way, but also in a musically homogenous way, so that the act is really a single movement with episodes, instead of being a succession of separate numbers, linked together... Puccini looks to me more like the heir of Verdi than any of his rivals.*

To add icing on the cake, the King of Italy decorated Puccini with the Order of the Cavalier's Cross.

The creative progress that Puccini made between *Edgar* and *Manon Lescaut* appears unfathomable, especially given the constant behind-the-scenes wrangling over the libretto. Yet to Puccini the situation seemed quite simple. Whereas with *Edgar* he struggled constantly to find ways of adapting his style to a dramatic template with which he felt ill-at-ease, in *Manon*'s case he made the libretto work for him, expanding upon those lyrical elements present in *Edgar* to create a more convincing and cohesive whole.

The stylistic changes in Puccini's creative personality are evident from the opening bars. There is no formal prelude, more an exuberant sense of forward momentum generated by the orchestra that hurtles the audience right into the action. The writing is playful and carefree; the orchestration is at once more colourful and individual, the range of expression wider, encompassing cantabile lyricism and staccato exuberance with the most subtle of emotional shadings.

When Des Grieux first emerges there is no grand entrance; instead, he seems almost insinuated into the musical textures: although he stands slightly apart from his friends, he is harmonically acknowledged by the music. As the carriage arrives carrying Manon, her brother and Geronte, the orchestra subtly conveys the scene using a multi-layered effect as the voices move in and out of dramatic focus. This is music in which the suggestion of a swoon from the orchestra speaks a thousand words. At times the vocal lines are little more than subtle forms of sung recitative, while the strings carry the melodic weight. Indeed, the entire first act creates the impression of one vast melodic edifice. As a result, when Des Grieux sings the very first set-piece aria, 'Donna non vidi'

Manon Lescaut

Act I: The curtain rises on the courtyard of an inn at Amiens towards the end of the eighteenth century. A crowd of students has assembled awaiting the arrival of a coach. The handsome Chevalier des Grieux, who is destined for the church, is teased by his male companions for not showing much interest in girls. That all changes with the arrival of the coach from which alights wealthy treasurer-general Geronte di Ravoir, along with Lescaut, a sergeant of the King's guards. Then comes Lescaut's sister, Manon, whom he is accompanying to the local convent; there she is to finish her education and take her vows, according to her parents' wishes. The moment Des Grieux sets eyes on Manon he is captivated by her natural grace and beauty. At the first opportunity he lets her know the intensity of his feelings and Manon, who although a loyal daughter is not really suited to celibate life, reciprocates them.

However, the ageing roué Geronte also has his eye on Manon and hatches a plan with the landlord (and with Lescaut's full co-operation) to abduct her from the inn that very evening. Fortunately Edmondo, a fellow student, overhears the dastardly plot and informs Des Grieux, who then persuades Manon to elope with him instead. At first the two older men are stunned by what has happened, but Lescaut assures Geronte that Manon's predilection for luxurious living is such that once this passing infatuation has worn off and the money has run out, she'll come begging to Geronte for forgiveness.

Act II: Lescaut's reading of his sister's taste for high living was correct – she is now living with Geronte in his lavish Paris apartments, having abandoned Des Grieux and their humble cottage home. Lescaut, a leech who has grown thoroughly accustomed to feeding off his sister's wealth, remains unrepentant over his selfish actions. Manon, in the first of Puccini's great heart-rending arias, 'In quelle trine morbide', reveals to him how desperately unhappy she is; but his one thought is how to get Des Grieux to make some fast money should Manon decide to leave him.

The atmosphere lightens in the charming scene in which Manon joins hands with the assembled company and performs a minuet as part of a dancing lesson. Her brother, meanwhile, finds Des Grieux and persuades him to go gambling in order to raise some money. Des Grieux goes on to win a considerable amount, makes straight for Manon at Geronte's house, and the two once again celebrate their feelings for each other in an impassioned love duet. When Geronte discovers them and sends for the police, Lescaut encourages the lovers to make a run for it; Manon won't leave without first collecting her jewels, much to Des Grieux's frustration. The delay proves their undoing: the gendarmerie arrest Manon on a trumped-up charge of being a coquette – her fate is deportation to Louisiana.

Act III: The famous orchestral intermezzo that precedes the act symbolises Manon's journey from Paris to Le Havre, her point of embarkation for America. Lescaut and Des Grieux have meanwhile hatched a desperate plan to rescue her from the harbour prison, but it is foiled at the last minute. The women are led out one by one, until Manon also emerges from the darkness, much to Des Grieux's consternation. Desperate not to be parted from his beloved, he earnestly pleads with the boat's captain to be taken on board no matter how lowly the position. The captain eventually relents and the boat sets sail.

Act IV: Set in the barren wilderness of an area of the Louisiana desert on the outskirts of New Orleans, night is falling as Des Grieux and Manon emerge exhausted on the scene, following yet another series of intrigues and skirmishes. This time any hope of a reprieve is useless – emotionally and physically shattered by everything that has happened, Manon is close to death. She begs Des Grieux to go and find some water while she sings of her desperate predicament in the soulful aria 'Sola, perduta, abbandonata'. When he returns Manon dies in his arms, declaring her love for him right to the end.

('I've never before seen such a woman'), it appears to grow entirely naturally out of and back into the music's rolling textures.

Because the music is literally continuous and sweeps along with a feeling of inevitability, there is a heightened sense of the drama being experienced in real time. Beginning the scene in which Geronte hatches his plan with the innkeeper to abscond with Manon, the music's texture changes – the vocal parts are written as melodic recitative while the orchestra gently comments. This delightful interlude moves the plot on with a velvet touch, and it makes the following love duet more devastating in its lyrical power and the scherzando writing that accompanies the lovers' swift exit all the more exhilarating.

Further evidence of the light years that Puccini had travelled since *Edgar* is provided by the opening of the second act which, in its light, fluffy orchestration and vocalising, succinctly captures the scene of Manon sitting down and being fussed-over by her hairdresser. Like their small talk, the music bubbles along undistractingly in a masterstroke of characterisation. Manon's aria, 'In quelle trine morbide' ('In these soft silken drapes'), in which she movingly confesses how cold the expensive furnishings seem by comparison with her short-lived dalliance with Des Grieux, sets the template for future confessional arias of its kind by Puccini. It starts simply, almost girlishly, rises in dramatic intensity to an explosive release, and falls back, not so much exhausted as reflective, returning us gently into the real world.

The famous Act III Intermezzo is contextually speaking the least convincing part of the entire work. The opening is rather too obviously influenced by Wagner's *Tristan und Isolde*, so the listener experiences a stylistic jolt when Puccini's unmistakable melodic radiance comes to the fore. Even the climax has a slightly hollow ring about it, a hint of sobbing hysteria that is pure *verismo*.

Far more convincing is the mood of gloomy despair that Puccini evokes as the act gets under way; it pervades much of what is to follow. This is the first of Puccini's brilliant crowd scenes that would reach fruition in the second act of *La Bohème*, and it is remarkable for sustaining a profoundly elegiac atmosphere through snippets of overlapping melody. The way in which the various layers intertwine, drifting in and out of focus, seems to anticipate similar techniques employed by Stravinsky during the Shrove-Tide Fair scene of his ballet *Petrushka* (1911).

At less than twenty minutes long, the fourth act feels relatively terse, opening with recollections from the string quartet *Crisantemi* that fit perfectly with the downcast mood. The finale as a whole caused Puccini endless problems due to its dramatic inactivity. Following the collage-like brilliance of the opening act, to end the work with the drawn-out demise of the central character was a considerable challenge. Puccini pulls it off – just. Yet one can see why he nervously excised Manon's big solo 'Sola, perduta, abbandonata' ('Alone, lost, abandoned') for a number of years before reinstating it in 1923, shortly before his own death.

Manon Lescaut doesn't entirely avoid minor-key hysteria, nor does it quite sustain the untrammelled melodic distinction of Puccini's later work. But Puccini's use of motifs is further extended – Manon introduces herself with a little falling phrase which returns, chromatically altered, when she lies exhausted in Act IV; a 'death' theme is also derived from the same figure. More than anything, the opera also pointed the way forward with a confidence, exuberance, and heart-rending sincerity that put most of Puccini's operatic contemporaries in the shade. Massenet's version is undeniably the more polished and subtly detailed work, yet Puccini's is fresher, more engaging, and it possesses an emotional thrust that Massenet's rarely even approaches.

If *Manon Lescaut* had moved Puccini's audiences uncontrollably to tears, his next opera would leave their emotions in tatters. This was only the beginning.

Chapter 5

His Master's Voice: *La Bohème*

His Master's Voice: *La Bohème*

No sooner had Puccini finished work on the score of *Manon Lescaut* than rumours began circulating that two composers were working independently on an operatic treatment of Henry Mürger's *Scènes de la vie de bohème* – Leoncavallo and Puccini. Both men were basking in the glory of their latest operatic successes (*I pagliacci* and *Manon Lescaut* respectively); both were living the high life on the proceeds and were also good friends. That was soon set to change.

While working on *Manon Lescaut* Puccini had toyed with a number of ideas for his next work. Again, Sardou's *La Tosca* was briefly considered and rejected; so was an idea for an opera based on *La lupa* ('The She-Wolf'), a short story by Giovanni Verga, whose writings had already inspired Mascagni's *Cavalleria rusticana*. What happened next is still a matter for conjecture. According to Puccini, he hit upon the idea of setting Mürger's story shortly after the premiere of *Manon Lescaut* and was flabbergasted to discover the following month during a now notorious encounter with Leoncavallo that the latter was already engaged on his own version. Leoncavallo insisted that the idea was entirely his and that Puccini had swiped it.

Whatever the truth of the matter, and Puccini's account is now generally accepted, there is no doubt that Leoncavallo was already hard at work on *La Bohème* using a libretto of his own devising (which he later claimed he had offered to Puccini the previous year, but had been turned down). At this stage Puccini was merely formulating musical ideas, while Illica and Giacosa – who initially had severe doubts about the story's suitability – worked respectively on the scenario and libretto.

Leoncavallo dealt the first public body-blow with the help of his publisher, Sonzogno. Two local newspapers carried a public declaration that Leoncavallo's next opera was to be *La Bohème*, that the composer had been working on it for several months (as

Leoncavallo in 1897

evidenced by the various parties involved), and that the opera would be ready the following year. Furthermore, Puccini had only recently thought of using the same story and therefore Leoncavallo had prior claim. It was left neatly implicit that Puccini was deliberately trying to spoil Leoncavallo's chances.

Puccini responded in an open letter with guile and cunning. Instead of a fusillade of robust denials and counter-accusations, he simply pointed out that Leoncavallo's announcement made it clear that there was no question of his having stolen the idea; in any case he would never have behaved this way towards someone he considered a close and dear friend. Then came the sting in the tail. 'However,' Puccini continued, 'for reasons that must be plain for all to see, things have changed irrevocably... Let him compose his opera, I shall compose mine and the public will be the judge.' In an attempt to prevent Leoncavallo from continuing, Ricordi tried to obtain the exclusive rights to Mürger's story only to discover that it had passed into the public domain and that legally there was nothing he could do. The race was on.

Behind the scenes the two composers remained on good speaking terms, and far from it turning into a first-past-the-post contest they appear to have continued as though there was no urgency at all. In Puccini's case this was due largely to his detailed fine-tuning of the libretto to his exact requirements, often replacing the work of seasoned literary professionals with his own prose, or timing the music dramatically to perfection and leaving it to the writers to come up with words to fit.

Illica and Giacosa had already experienced innumerable frustrations in working on *Manon Lescaut* and neither relished going another ten rounds with the composer on the new work. This spills over in a letter from Illica to Ricordi, written in a tone of mock-exasperation shortly before Illica rolled up his sleeves for serious work on *La Bohème*.

> *I often end up groping around in the darkness, searching here and there for that special 'something' that Puccini requires, only to be invariably told that 'I don't like it'; as a result I run the risk of ending up where we left off with* Manon, *using his lines of doggerel verse.*

Having unfavourably compared their collaboration with that of Verdi and Boito, and complained about Puccini's constant vacillating over whether or not to choose *Tosca* as a subject instead, Illica implored Ricordi to intervene and encourage

Puccini to keep to what he did best: composing. Nothing could be done, however, and although Illica and Giacosa would eventually tire of the situation, at this point they put a brave face on things and bore with the maestro's indecision.

First they had to catch him. A rough first draft of the libretto was ready by the early summer, but Puccini was now proving decidedly elusive. As revisions continued with the libretto, the hunting season had started at Torre del Lago, from where Puccini boasted of 'killing hundreds of birds' and invited Illica to join him. He offered the following 'inducement':

> *In my house there are soft beds, chickens, geese, ducks, lambs, fleas, tables, chairs, guns, paintings, statues, shoes, velocipedes, pianos, sewing machines, clocks, a map of Paris, good oil, fish, three different types of wine (we don't drink water), cigars, hammocks, wife [strictly speaking not true], children, dogs, cats, coffee, different kinds of pasta, a can of rotten sardines, peas, figs, two outhouses, a eucalyptus, a well in the house and a broom – all for you (except the wife). Come.*

There were also performances of *Manon Lescaut* to prepare and attend both at home and abroad, in between which Puccini advised on revisions to the libretto. Meanwhile he showed not the slightest inclination to start composing.

Inevitably the writers began to feel like lackeys, constantly pulling literary rabbits out of the hat while Puccini was off shooting and covering himself in glory as Italy's young operatic genius. It was Giacosa who first began to show signs of strain in the midsummer heat. He was an internationally recognised figure in his own right and therefore had important commitments of his own. Additionally he was a devoted family man with a sensitive nature that made him more of a perfectionist than Illica, the world-weary realist.

By October 1893 Giacosa had had enough and wanted to withdraw, citing what would become the second act as his main source of concern. Finding it dramatically unworkable, he had gradually become worn down by the pall of gloom that he felt pervaded the entire work. What he had originally envisaged as a relatively light-hearted piece that would turn to tragedy only at the end had, he felt, become overbearingly morose. Additionally, given his high intellectual pedigree and cultured background, he found the 'earthy' characters both unsympathetic and unpalatable. The story, essentially, had no 'depth', so Giacosa failed to see what a man of his profound gifts could bring to it.

Giacosa's formal resignation came as a bitter blow to Ricordi, yet there was worse to come. Concerned by the lack of progress on the libretto, Puccini decided to put a spanner of his own in the works, claiming to be fast losing interest in the project altogether. This was the spark that lit the touchpaper of Ricordi's negotiating genius. Spurred on by Illica's insistence that whatever happened they simply couldn't give Leoncavallo the pleasure of a clear shot at the story ('it is now a matter of personal honour,' he insisted), somehow Ricordi got both Puccini and Giacosa back on side by January 1894.

It was now a year since Illica had first set to work on adapting Mürger's story: the libretto was still far from ready and Puccini had written very little, a situation that looked unlikely to change as he set off to supervise more productions of *Manon Lescaut*. A revival in Naples went so well that he stayed on for three performances before travelling to Milan. Although the opera was generally well received by the public, Puccini was suffering from one of his characteristic winter depressions and he could find hardly a good word to say for it, memorably encapsulating the entire production as a 'stagnant Dead Sea'. A spot of hunting and a brief visit to Lucca followed, to see Catalani's ashes interred. Catalani, like Puccini a native of Lucca, had finally achieved operatic success with *La Wally* (to a libretto by Illica) but succumbed aged thirty-nine to the effects of tuberculosis which had plagued him all his life. His relationship with Puccini was troubled – he had been jealous of the success of *Manon Lescaut* and the confirmation it brought that Puccini was the operatic heir to Verdi. Later, Puccini arrived in Pisa to see the great Arturo Toscanini in action and then went on to Budapest to hear the celebrated Hungarian conductor, Artur Nikisch. Vienna, Munich and Covent Garden, London followed in quick succession.

Clearly the burgeoning success of *Manon Lescaut* was of vital importance in establishing Puccini's name, as well as providing an income for the likes of Ricordi, Illica and Giacosa. Yet while Puccini had been gallivanting off around Italy and Europe, there had been continuing problems with the libretto, and this time it was Illica who was nearing the end of his tether. He complained bitterly about the contentious second-act crowd scenes in the Latin Quarter, waspishly pointing out that 'There is no one as blind as one who will not see [i.e. Puccini]', and that 'there is no one more impossible to please than someone who takes pleasure in making others work while he does little himself'. Clearly Puccini's absenteeism was beginning to take its toll, and now that Illica was due to start work on preparing a libretto for an opera on *Tosca* – this time with the composer Alberto Franchetti – time was increasingly of the essence.

Even at this stage, Puccini, during a trip to Sicily, managed to muddy the waters by reconsidering the possibility of returning to *La lupa* in preference to *La Bohème*. Ricordi remained a model of patience and understanding, but Puccini realised that this time he had gone too far. Ricordi had given his 'chosen one' a longer leash than any composer (and his librettists) could reasonably wish for, and in return all he seemed to get was insurrection and sparring from within the ranks. Ricordi's chief publishing rival Sonzogno had recently brought out two smash hits (Leoncavallo's *Pagliacci* and Mascagni's *Cavalleria rusticana*), and, for all Ricordi knew, Leoncavallo's *La Bohème* could well be another one.

Puccini finally got down to work, yet even now his efforts seemed piecemeal and lacking in the kind of commitment Ricordi was looking for. Illica then decided he had had enough of being pushed around by Puccini as though he were 'a dog' and threatened resignation. After a torrent of correspondence Ricordi the peacemaker prevailed once again. There were still many months of revisions ahead, but by the end of August Illica had produced a full libretto that met with Puccini's approval. The composer meanwhile claimed to have sketched out much of the music for Act I, keeping himself going with vast quantities of cigarettes and strong coffee. A delightful piano miniature entitled *Piccolo valzer*, composed around this time for the launching of a Genoese battleship, would later be adapted as Musetta's waltz song in Act II.

Matters seemed to be improving, not least Puccini's general mood. During the summer of 1894 he became a fully accepted citizen of Torre del Lago where he was able to indulge his various passions. The world he had entered into was less a traditional man's world than one replete with big boy's games. He set up shop in a run-down wooden hut by the lakeside where he would invite friends around to gamble, play cards, drink, eat and be merry. He even formed a makeshift organisation known as the 'Bohème Club' of which he became the honorary president. Almost as though he were playing out a role in his latest opera he devised a set of daft, knockabout rules which must have gone down uproariously with a few draughts of ale inside its members. Article 6 declared that 'it is forbidden to play cards honestly', Article 7 that 'silence is prohibited', and Article 8 that 'wisdom is not permitted, except in special cases'. All harmless, jolly japes that helped the composer relax – and distract him from his work. However, little by little the opera progressed until, as if by magic, on 12 January 1895 everyone declared themselves reasonably happy with the completed first draft and on 25 January Puccini set to work on orchestrating the first act.

The remainder of the year was almost entirely taken up with knocking *La Bohème* into something like its final form. Scenes were dropped (particularly from the final act), others added, while Giacosa nearly pulled out again – the third act looked as though it might overwhelm him, following countless revisions insisted upon by the composer. Finally, 10 December saw the culmination of three years' work with the death of Mimì; this so deeply affected Puccini that he wept openly, 'as though a child of my own had died'. Exhausted but elated, he went out with the locals to celebrate.

That *La Bohème* is the product of a cycle of disputes, disagreements, misunderstandings, laziness and sheer stubbornness can hardly be doubted. The third act nearly didn't make it into the mix, and the virtuoso triumph that is Act II was almost abandoned on several occasions due to the difficulties in making an act (which includes wild street scenes as well as more intimate and emotionally crucial interior scenes) work both musically and dramatically. Nevertheless, the opera flows with an ease and inevitability, creating the impression that it was somehow composed in one effortless flow of sublime inspiration. The story as Puccini finally set it drew from him an impassioned masterpiece that in many ways he never surpassed – the reason being that, more than in any other of Puccini's operas, and in spite of the differences in society then and now, we can identify fully with the

Part of Puccini's handwritten score of La Bohème; *a skull and crossbones marks the point where Mimì dies*

characters; anyone who has loved and lost while living in debt in a cold student flat, or who has shed a tear over a friend who died young, or needlessly, will share the bohemians' feelings.

The premiere of *La Bohème* was planned for Turin, exactly three years after *Manon Lescaut*'s triumph. This time there was no chance of obtaining a La Scala opening night as the theatre was now managed by Ricordi's great publishing rival, Sonzogno. A reliable if hardly starry cast was assembled in Turin and during January Puccini supervised musical rehearsals under Toscanini's baton, while Illica looked after stage business. There were concerns that the chosen Rodolfo wouldn't last the full two hours, while Marcello turned out to be a dreadfully wooden actor. Heated telegrams passed back and forth between Puccini and Ricordi, but in the end everyone held their nerve and the premiere went ahead as planned on 1 February 1896.

Although hardly a disaster, the initial response to Puccini's latest masterwork was a shade subdued. There was warm applause for Rodolfo's 'Che gelida manina' and Puccini took three curtain calls at the end of Act I. More curtain calls followed, particularly at the very end; but by Italian standards of the time, especially bearing in mind that *La Bohème* would before long become one of the most widely performed operas in history, it was a cautious start. Part of the problem was that local audiences were still in the grip of Wagner fever following a recent performance of a very different kind of work: *Götterdämmerung*. Puccini's *Bohème* moved along with such conversational ease – the very opposite of Wagner's grand declamations. In addition, there was the fast pace and intricacy of Act II, which for some came over as a hectic muddle, to say nothing of the third act's 'oriental' harmonies.

'It will leave a scant trace in the history of opera,' wrote Carlo Berzesio famously in the local *Gazetta piemontese*, 'and

the author would be well advised to consider it a passing error.'
The Turin critic for the *Gazetta del popolo* felt that Puccini
had simply gone off the rails:

> *We ask ourselves what has pushed Puccini along this
> deplorable road of* Bohème. *The question is a severe one, and
> we do not pose it without pain, we who have applauded and
> are still applauding* Manon, *which revealed a composer who
> knew how to marry orchestral mastery with an Italian feeling.
> Maestro, you are young and strong. You have talent, culture
> and imagination such as few possess. Today you have made
> the public applaud where and when you wanted. For this
> once, let us say no more about it, but in the future return to
> the great and difficult battles of art.*

Visiting critics were a great deal more complimentary, and
despite reservations about the 'troublesome' second act the
general feeling was that Puccini would soon have another hit
on his hands. And they were right. As audiences adjusted to
what Puccini had actually written rather than what they had
expected, the floodgates of enthusiasm opened. Within three
years the work had become an operatic sensation, having
travelled successfully to (in order) Buenos Aires, Alexandria,
Moscow, Lisbon, Manchester, Berlin, Rio de Janeiro, Mexico,
London, Vienna, Los Angeles, The Hague, Prague, Barcelona,
Athens, New York, Paris, Malta, Valparaiso, Warsaw, Zagreb,
Smyrna (now Izmir), Helsinki, St Petersburg and Algiers.

In the short term, however, it was the major Italian centres
that most concerned Puccini. Once Rome had recovered from
the novel quality of the first two acts it was totally won over,
as were Sicily and Naples. Most gratifying was the reception
in Palermo in March 1896. Ricordi had made sure that the
work received much local publicity, as usual, but nothing had

prepared the composer for the reception of the opera itself. At the end there was total pandemonium as the audience cried and shouted its hysterical approval. There were curtain calls galore lasting well over half an hour – yet still the public wanted more. In the end the singers, some of whom had already changed out of their costumes, had little choice but to return to the stage to redeliver the crushing final scene. Only then was everyone allowed to go home. Puccini had never witnessed anything like it.

Leoncavallo's *La Bohème* appeared in 1897, and although it is by any standards a fine work, written with great skill and dramatic flair (with the focus more on the Musetta–Marcello relationship), it ultimately lacks the sheer memorability of Puccini's version. With Leoncavallo one feels an observer of events; with Puccini one is propelled along with the characters as though on an emotional helter-skelter. After being initially well received, Leoncavallo's opera never quite recovered from being 'second past the post' in the public's eyes.

Puccini's *La Bohème*, on the other hand, is such a vital and familiar part of operatic life that it is easy to take for granted its unique qualities. The infectious skip of the opening section (derived from the *Capriccio sinfonico* of 1883) sets an exuberant tone that refuses to settle until just before Marcello's first entry. This deftly handled opening leaves the audience with the impression that the action has been going on for some time. Marcello's first utterance is mock formal recitative, highlighting the fact that Puccini's music actually flows with the ease of a musical conversation.

Music and drama integrate seamlessly in a way that may appear Wagnerian in its cohesiveness, yet the music proceeds with a sleight-of-hand nonchalance that the German composer rarely achieved. As we've seen, Puccini had already used Wagner's leitmotif techniques – whereby certain characters, objects and emotions become associated with specific musical motifs – in all three of his previous operas. Yet in *La Bohème* the method is used with developing subtlety. The music linked with Rodolfo's carefree existence, for example, is brought into the unforgettable 'Che gelida manina' ('Your tiny hand is frozen') later in the first act. However, it is now at a slower tempo and exquisitely transformed in a way that suggests Rodolfo becoming a caring lover in front of our eyes. He is, both actually and musically, giving himself to Mimì, who responds with her beautiful and famous aria 'Mi chiamano Mimì' ('They call me Mimì').

Throughout this opening scene Puccini achieves a perfect fusion of conversational speech and music by adopting, musically speaking, the vernacular. That these are, after all, ordinary people made extraordinary by their context is reflected with music of a deceptive, nursery-rhyme simplicity. This reaches its apogee with Schaunard's entrance, which is made to music with a fast skip in its gait. This has the effect of emphasising the child within; in a way, Puccini has taken us back to childhood through music of almost playground singability. As a result Rodolfo and Mimì's first encounter seems all the more overwhelming – like the first awakening of feelings which neither previously suspected they were capable of.

Act II sustains this child-like vision of the world in more spectacular fashion: in a sense the area around the Café Momus becomes an adult playground, the appearance of the puppet master deliberately blurring the distinction between actual children and those who merely behave like children. All of this is, of course, a brilliant ploy to settle us into a world of blissful simplicity before the tragedy of the opera's second half begins to unfold. It is also worth noting the symmetry of Puccini's vision – Acts I & II and III & IV both typically play for fifty-five minutes per pair.

In another inspired moment of musical symbolism Puccini sets Musetta's big aria 'Quando me'n vo' soletta per la via' ('As I wander the streets alone') as a waltz; the dancing of the first act therefore continues, only we have moved from the playground into the heated fragrance of barely suppressed sexuality that was the nineteenth-century ballroom. As Rodolfo and Mimì's love for each other deepens, so the music symbolises sexual awakening. Most remarkable of all, however, is the way in which Puccini has sustained a mood of unquenchable optimism for nearly an hour; the second act is a masterpiece of exuberance as well as one of intricate stage management. Puccini offsets this passage with a little piece of comic interplay between Alcindoro and Musetta. 'Ahi!' Musetta cries out in mock agony at her footwear; 'Che c'è'? ('What is it now?') enquires the exasperated Alcindoro.

Puccini conjures up an entirely different atmosphere with the opening of the third act. Up until this point his orchestration has tended towards the pungent and opulent, but now it is delicate, almost pointillist in its transparency and delicacy. The harmonic language has also changed, the parallel 5ths in the flutes falling like oriental snowflakes. Puccini is still playing with multiple musical personalities, however. While the orchestra sets the chilliness of the scene, Musetta is heard recalling her waltz from inside the inn, while the gathered merchants and peasants stand at the gates to the city. The strings enter with Mimì's song but are cut short – the warmth in her heart has been gradually overcome by the chill in her body as tuberculosis takes hold. Snatches of melody from the previous two acts continually drift in and out of the musical fabric; that Rodolfo and Mimì find life together impossible at times yet cannot live without each other is once again masterfully suggested as the music subtly refracts and changes colour.

La Bohème

Act I: It is Christmas Eve in Paris, in around 1830. The mood is carefree and playful as the poet Rodolfo and painter Marcello in their Latin Quarter garret keep themselves warm by throwing pages from the first act of Rodolfo's latest opus on to the fire. They are joined by their friend Colline, a young philosopher who has unsuccessfully attempted to pawn some books. Another act goes on the fire, providing a suitably warm glow. Two young men suddenly enter, followed closely by the last member of the quartet, the musician Schaunard, who has spent three days working for an eccentric English gentleman, resulting in enough food, fuel and money to keep them going for a while. Rodolfo locks the door and the four settle down to relax with a glass of wine. Schaunard suggests that as it is Christmas they should repair to their favourite drinking-hole, the Café Momus.

However, they are halted in their tracks by a knock at the door – it is Benoit, their landlord, chasing some long overdue rent. Encouraged by the sight of Schaunard's money on the table Benoit relaxes, has a glass of wine and starts to boast of his extra-marital conquests. Feigning indignation, the four comrades eject him from the room without paying him one sou. As the others go to leave as planned, Rodolfo stays behind to finish off a magazine article.

A timid knock at the door signals the entrance of Mimì, a young embroiderer whose candle has gone out. As Rodolfo goes to assist, the resulting draught also extinguishes his candle and as the two fumble about in the dark their hands touch. 'Your tiny hand is frozen,' he sings exultantly, to which she responds no less movingly with 'They call me Mimì'. The two form an instant bond and leave to join Rodolfo's companions at the café.

Act II: The curtain rises on the main avenue intersection where the Café Momus is situated; the mood is one of excited anticipation of the Christmas celebrations. Rodolfo and Mimì are strolling hand-in-hand, Colline is standing outside a tailor's shop, Schaunard is haggling over some trinket, Marcello is struggling to find a path through the jostling crowd, and all the time street vendors are vying for attention as people from all walks of life pass by.

As the scene progresses snippets of chorus, recitative and orchestral accompaniment move in and out of focus as various calls, shouts and café orders are heard rising above the general hubbub. Rodolfo buys Mimì a new bonnet and the two finally join their friends at a café table. Parpignol the toy vendor passes by, followed by a throng of admiring children as the five settle down to a night of wine, women and song. Enter Musetta, a larger-than-life character who openly flirts as she sings a memorable waltz-song, all the time attended by her aged admirer, the state councillor Alcindoro – although it is into the arms of her lover Marcello that she eventually falls. A military tattoo is heard in the distance and as the six friends depart to take a closer look, the hapless Alcindoro is left to pick up the tab.

Act III: Dawn on the outskirts of Paris, where a crowd of people are standing at a toll gate (the Barrière d'Enfer – 'Hell's Gate') in the February snow, waiting for permission to enter the city. The sound of revelry is heard from a nearby tavern. Mimì enters, wracked by coughing fits and clearly in serious need of medical attention. She has come to see Marcello and Musetta to tell them that she has decided to leave Rodolfo as she can no longer cope with his uncontrollable jealousy. She hides as Rodolfo emerges from the tavern and tells Marcello that he cannot cope with his and Mimì's constant quarrelling, and feels he must part from her. However, he finally breaks down and reveals the real reason – his desperate concern about her failing health, which he cannot afford to do anything about. Mimì emerges from her hiding place and the two resolve to stay together at least until the spring, while in the background the lively sounds of Musetta and Marcello having a lovers' tiff can clearly be heard.

Act IV: Set some months later back in the garret room familiar from Act I. Rodolfo and Marcello console each other over the departure of their respective beloveds as Schaunard and Colline arrive with a few scraps to sustain them. To raise their spirits the four begin a mock dance which quickly escalates into general tomfoolery. Just as it seems as though all is right with the world again, Musetta bursts in and announces that Mimì is close to death and wishes to spend her remaining hours with Rodolfo and his friends. Rodolfo carries in Mimì who is clearly not long for this world. Musetta hands her earrings to Marcello and sends him off to buy some medicine, while Colline dashes off in the hope of selling his overcoat. Musetta then leaves to get her muff to help keep Mimì warm. Rodolfo and Mimì, now alone, gently reflect on happier times before their friends return to offer what little help they can. However, it is too late. Rodolfo collapses sobbing, crying out his beloved's name with inconsolable anguish.

The final act initially takes up where the first left off, but is now interposed with lyrical music of surpassing beauty. In 'Sono andati?' ('Are we alone?') Mimì and Rodolfo recall happier days together. This is more than mere nostalgia – the music reveals that while the characters are in many ways the same, they have been irrevocably changed by all that has happened. Like the tide, the music surges and recedes, tantalisingly suggesting the uncertainty as to what may happen. Mimì's spirits even appear

to revive as she recalls her first encounter with Rodolfo in 'La mia cuffietta' ('My little bonnet'). Will Mimì survive after all? No matter how many times one has seen *La Bohème*, and no matter how certain one is that Mimì will indeed die, there is still a profound sense of shock when it actually happens. Puccini gives us hope up to the last second, making us share Rodolfo's sense of disbelief with a raw intensity. For those who truly surrender to the opera at this point, it can be one of the most shattering of musical experiences.

Puccini's *La Bohème* might well have become an early, brilliant success which he struggled to match for the rest of his career. His ability, however, to produce operas at the highest level time and again is testimony not only to his powers of invention but of reinvention. At times during *La Bohème*'s creation Puccini may have appeared lazy, disinterested even, yet he never once countenanced the idea of retiring and living off the profits accrued by *Manon* and *Bohème* – financially speaking a very real option at this time. He did, however, buy outright his old family home in Lucca (although he had no intention of living there), also a luxurious yacht proudly named *Mimì I*, and began drawing up plans for a new residence in Torre del Lago. And during these early months of seeing *La Bohème* safely onto the boards Puccini was also thinking about his next project – which this time would be a thriller straight out of the *verismo* copybook.

Chapter 6

Verismo Shocker:
Tosca

"
All the time he chiselled away, often
long into the night when it was
cooler, changing little musical details
here, a line or two there, gradually
honing the music until it
was shorn of all excess.
"

Verismo Shocker: *Tosca*

At the time that Puccini had first considered Tosca as a possible subject for operatic treatment (while working on revisions for *Edgar* in 1889), his source was virtually hot off the press. Victorien Sardou's play *La Tosca* had been written for Sarah Bernhardt and premiered on 24 November 1887. Sardou was then at the height of his fame, his plays renowned more for their visceral impact than profound literary depth. His advice to young playwrights hungry for success was simple: 'Torture the women!' It was George Bernard Shaw who in a less than admiring article on Sardou's work in 1895 coined the term 'Sardoodledum'.

Sardou's *La Tosca* was a theatrical sensation and Puccini had attended a couple of performances, egged on by his then librettist Fontana. Even after being overlooked for both *Manon Lescaut* and *La Bohème*, Fontana continued to badger Ricordi about his being the man to work with Puccini on *Tosca* – it was, after all, he who had initially suggested the idea to the composer. Ricordi was not swayed, however, and Fontana was never in the frame as librettist.

Puccini saw immediately that *La Tosca* would provide him with the perfect vehicle free of the bloated set pieces and epic sweep that he had found so unconducive when working on both *Le villi* and *Edgar*. First he had to gain the rights from Sardou, and the delicate task of persuading him was entrusted to Emanuele Muzzio, Verdi's top man in Paris. Sardou, if nothing else, was a businessman and was certainly not prepared to let his work go for a song. Eventually agreement was reached, but not before Puccini was busy working on *La Bohème*. Ricordi nevertheless proceeded to ask Illica to prepare a scenario and then a full libretto in collaboration with Alberto Franchetti (1860–1942), a composer strongly influenced by Meyerbeer and Wagner.

Things didn't run smoothly from the start. Illica had constant problems wrestling the story around to Franchetti's satisfaction, while

Victorien Sardou

Franchetti, having completed the first act, became increasingly convinced that the more explicitly nasty elements in the story were beyond his musical vocabulary. He was also aware that Puccini, disappointed to have lost such a promising scenario, was being kept in touch with developments. In the end Franchetti appears to have washed his hands of the project. For many years it was assumed that Ricordi had put pressure on Franchetti to give up *Tosca* until a recently discovered letter made plain the publisher's displeasure at Franchetti's resignation.

Whatever the truth of the matter, in August 1895, six months before the Turin premiere of *La Bohème*, Puccini had declared enthusiastically to a friend that Illica's libretto, which compressed Sardou's original five acts into three, looked like an exciting prospect. From this point onwards there was never any serious doubt that *Tosca* would be Puccini's next operatic venture, even if it would be another four and a half

CD 2 [1]–[5]

website

years before the curtain rose on the work's premiere in Rome. The definitive scenario for Puccini's *Tosca* was still some time in the future, yet the essence of Illica's first adaptation clearly indicates the extraordinary potential that the composer saw in Sardou's play; the stark differences between the story's graphic brutality and the essentially gentle disposition of *La Bohème* were also underlined.

From the beginning Giacosa had serious doubts about the story. For a start, he wondered how he was supposed to make anything out of a first act so full of detail and incident. As he rightly pointed out, it was impossible to drop anything from the scenario without destroying the sense of what was happening. Yet despite these issues Act I was ready within a month, although Puccini found some of it overwritten – too literary. This was like a red rag to a bull, and before long Giacosa was once again on the point of resigning, complaining that he had already worked a miracle in producing anything from a work so completely unsuited to poetic adaptation. Eventually calming down, and with Ricordi becoming increasingly impatient with his outbursts of temperament, Giacosa had the entire first draft ready by the end of the year.

Up to this point Puccini had typically done very little work of his own on the score, and with his diary for 1897 already full with important first performances of *La Bohème*, there seemed to be little chance of this changing. However, it seems that he applied himself whenever he had the opportunity; despite the usual social distractions (including the inevitable hunting), by the end of the year Puccini was in Rome researching the sounds of church bells and ensuring that all ecclesiastical references in *Tosca* were authentic.

On the domestic front matters were more settled, with Elvira and her daughter Fosca ensconced at Torre del Lago, and Tonio attending boarding school. During this period

Puccini found time to compose two song settings: *Avanti,
Urania!* and *Inno a Diana*, potboilers of no great distinction,
the latter being marginally the fresher and more memorable
of the two. By the end of the year the music for *Tosca* was also
in draft form, and according to the autograph score Puccini
began orchestrating the first act in January 1898.

Later that year there were meetings with Sardou himself
and then the Paris premiere of *La Bohème* on 13 June at
the Opéra Comique. It delighted the audience yet, typically,
left the critics less than enthusiastic, including one who
described Puccini's cherishable melodies as 'banal'. Stifled by
the formality of city life, Puccini was becoming increasingly
desperate for the simple pleasures of home:

> *I am sick of Paris! I am panting for the fragrant woods, for the
> free movement of my belly in wide trousers and no waistcoat;
> I pant after the wind that blows free and fragrant from the
> sea; I savour with wide nostrils its salty breath and expand
> my lungs to breathe it! I hate pavements! I hate palaces! I hate
> capitals! I hate columns! I love the beautiful column of the
> poplar and the fir; I love the vault of shady glades; and I love,
> like a modern druid, to make my temple, my house, my studio
> therein! I love the green expanse of cool shelter in forest old or
> young; I love the blackbird, blackcap, the woodpecker! I hate
> the horse, the cat, the house sparrow and the toy dog! I hate
> the steamer, the top hat and the dress coat!*

With money plentiful following *La Bohème*'s success, Puccini
began developing his property portfolio. By the summer,
work was already underway on a luxury villa in the remote
village of Chiatra, which he had happy memories of visiting
when he was a child. He became extremely fond of the area,
often returning to compose there away from the bright city

lights of Milan. But for now he continued to refine *Tosca* in the unpleasantly sultry climate of a mountain retreat called Monsagrati, near Celle.

All the time he chiselled away, often long into the night when it was cooler, changing little musical details here, a line or two there, gradually honing the music until it was shorn of all excess. For a Romantic composer whose instincts were to luxuriate and let music breathe naturally, unhindered and free, this kind of discipline was especially challenging. The winter was spent back in Milan, where typically Puccini felt ill at ease with the trappings of celebrity, the constant interruptions and the sheer nervous pace of city life.

By January 1899, the broken rhythms of his existence had begun seriously to impair his creativity, so it was with some relief that he made his way to Paris and met Sardou to discuss certain aspects of the final act. Then it was back to Milan via the gambling tables of Monte Carlo, and during February (more than a year after starting the orchestration of Act I) he began fleshing out the instrumentation of the second act. The summer saw work progress on Act III through to completion, although personal sadness struck when Elvira suffered a miscarriage.

Up until this point Puccini had never needed to worry about Ricordi's opinion of his music. The first two acts of *Tosca* had been warmly received by his publisher, but when Puccini sent him Act III in September 1899 Ricordi was not at all pleased. In a letter to the composer he expressed his severe disappointment, particularly as regards the central duet. He found it so lacking in emotional power, freshness and melodic distinction that he felt it was in severe danger of sinking the entire work. Ricordi was also dismayed that what he described as the 'flabby, rather ordinary melody' accorded the passage beginning

'O dolci mani' ('Oh sweet hands') had been lifted straight out of *Edgar*.

Puccini had not even remotely anticipated this and was deeply hurt by Ricordi's reservations, mounting a firm defence in a letter of 11 October. Referring to the duet, he pointed out that its fragmentary nature was entirely intended. 'This cannot be executed in the normal manner of love duets, all smooth and tranquil,' he insisted. 'Tosca's thoughts are continually interrupted by her concern that Mario should fall convincingly and that his feigning of death should appear convincing in front of a firing squad.' Having rebuffed Ricordi's detailed observations (blaming much on 'the poets'), he offered to come to Milan immediately and discuss the act in detail at the piano. In the event Ricordi backed down and Act III stayed exactly as Puccini had originally intended. The two men would never cross swords in this way again.

Given the opera's location it was inevitable that Rome was chosen as the venue for *Tosca*'s premiere. A first-rate cast was assembled for curtain-up on 14 January 1900 at the Teatro Constanzi, under the distinguished conductor Leopoldo Mugnone, and the celebrity audience included royalty, various other dignitaries and several fellow composers. It was a truly national event that provoked the highest degree of anticipation and excitement. Ricordi's son, Tito, had ensured that no one attended the rehearsals; apart from the subject matter, the audience had not the slightest idea of what to expect on the night.

As if Mugnone hadn't already enough to contend with, fifteen minutes before he was due to go on he received a warning from the police. There was the real possibility that a bomb might be thrown during the performance, in which case he was to direct the orchestra to play the national anthem. Mugnone would have taken this warning extremely seriously, as at this time Italy was in the throes of political instability, and there had recently been two unsuccessful attempts on the life of King Umberto II. Just as the performance was about to begin there was a mild disturbance in the stalls caused, as it turned out, by latecomers upsetting those already in their seats. Poor Mugnone brought the premiere to a brief halt and then started again. The rest of the performance passed without further upset.

The initial excitement generated by the 'bomb' incident appears to have sharpened the audience's dramatic appetite. Several numbers had to be repeated before the performance was allowed to continue, Cavaradossi's 'E lucevan le stelle' in particular; having already been encored, this aria caused such delight that Puccini was called up on stage several times before the audience would settle again. That said, the overall response was enthusiastic rather than overwhelming. Even the gruesome spectacle of the second act failed to have the audience fainting in the aisles quite as Puccini had hoped. However, opera lovers quickly caught on to the work's brutish novelty and fully embraced the macabre elements; there was a series of sell-out performances, not just in Italy but – before the year was out – in England, the United States and South America. As had become his habit, Puccini attended the rehearsals for a number of early premieres to see his new musical offspring safely into the world, including those at La Scala under Toscanini and at Covent Garden.

The critics were predictably less than impressed, one dismissing the work as 'three hours of sheer noise' (perhaps this just seemed to be the case, as *Tosca* plays for only two hours). Puccini's orchestration and melodic writing were in general admired, although the cognoscenti were taken aback by the graphic violence of much of the writing. Perhaps the most balanced review came from Ippolito Valetta in the *Nuovo*

Hariclea Darclée, who created the role of Tosca at the Teatro Constanzi in Rome, 1900

antologia. He praised Puccini for the sophistication of his technique and subtle use of orchestral colour, even if he took exception to the 'many successions of fourths, huge delays in the resolutions of dissonances, rapid transitions through curious modulations, contrasts of rhythm, syncopations, and strong accents on the weak beats of the bar'. Gabriel Fauré, one of the few discerning voices of his time to speak kindly of Puccini's work on occasion, also objected to the 'frightful brutalities' of *Tosca*. Later on the American musicologist Joseph Kerman famously described the opera as a 'shabby little shocker'.

No work of Puccini's has come in for such vitriolic censure as *Tosca*. There is indeed an air of nerve-jangling hysteria and imposing physicality about both the action and (often) Puccini's music that is certainly not for the faint-hearted. Whereas in *La Bohème* broad brushstrokes of mood are coloured and highlighted by passing inflections that gently coalesce into the textures, in *Tosca* a quick-fire emotional changeability in the music captures the tautness and the speed of activity (particularly in the opening act). Just as surely as Puccini matched the playground antics of his bohemians with nursery-rhyme sing-song in *La Bohème*, so in *Tosca* the hard-edged, volatile action is reflected in choppy, short-breathed musical motifs.

Tosca's famous opening manages to be both unsettling and ominous: in just three chords Puccini moves from B flat to a remote E major. Throughout the opera these chords come to represent the forces of evil in general, or more specifically the opera's devil incarnate: Scarpia. The music then hurtles away, the syncopated cross-beats perfectly suggesting the fugitive Angelotti's plight as he bursts into the church. Puccini's ingenuity knows no bounds here. So far we have no sense of what key we are in, or of a regular pulse, and the style and patterning of the music refuses to relax. Only when the Sacristan enters does Puccini allow some form of respite, with a warm glow of certainty enveloping the music's high spirits. Here is a man as uncomplicated and grounded as the music that surrounds him. Puccini gently jibes at the Sacristan by setting his world-weariness against music of sparkling optimism and jauntiness – witness his startled 'Sante ampolle!' (literally 'Holy cruets!') where he recognises the woman in Cavaradossi's portrait as one of his regular parishioners. As Cavaradossi sings 'Recondita armonia' ('The mysterious similarities') it is not just the subject matter (comparing the woman in his portrait with his beloved Tosca) that feels inappropriate in a church: the music, too, becomes worldly, opulent and harmonically indulgent.

Following the warm, flowing lines of her duet with Cavaradossi, it becomes obvious that Tosca is a very different animal from Mimì. Here is a formidable personality, who in just a few minutes rolls out a whole range of human emotions from suspicion through tenderness and affection to raging jealousy, playfulness and unbridled passion. It is one of the great soprano scenes, for not only must the singer convey the many varieties of mood through her voice, she has to act well while maintaining complete credibility. When Angelotti re-emerges, the musical atmosphere subtly changes to something altogether more engagingly lyrical than before. Events have moved on and Cavaradossi is no longer surprised to see his old friend.

The mood darkens at the mention of Scarpia, but, even as the cannon sounds, Puccini sweeps us away with the Sacristan and choir rejoicing in their good fortune of extra money for the evening's *Te Deum*. Quite unexpectedly, Scarpia's menacing motif rips through the orchestral texture when he is seen glowering in the doorway. As Scarpia begins to unravel everything that has passed in the last half-hour, the atmosphere

Tosca

Act I: In Rome, 17 June 1800 – three days after the Battle of Marengo. Cesare Angelotti, a political prisoner who has escaped from the Castel Sant'Angelo, bursts into the Church of Sant'Andrea della Valle. He is a former consul of Rome now being hunted by his Neapolitan oppressors. Half crazed, he sees a statue of the Madonna at the foot of which he finds a key left by his sister and, letting himself into the Attavanti Chapel, disappears from view. The Sacristan wanders in, and is surprised to find an easel but no painter. As the Angelus rings out and the Sacristan kneels in prayer, the artist Mario Cavaradossi enters. As Cavaradossi pulls back the covers from the portrait of Mary Magdalene that he has been working on, the Sacristan disapprovingly notices her resemblance to a lady who has frequently visited the church to pray (Angelotti's sister). The painter seems unconcerned, however, and in 'Recondita armonia' lovingly compares the blonde image in the portrait with his own dark-haired beloved, celebrated singer Floria Tosca.

After the Sacristan leaves, Angelotti comes out of hiding and is relieved to recognise Cavaradossi as an old friend. Their reunion is short-lived, however, as Tosca is heard outside calling the painter's name. Cavaradossi sends Angelotti back into the chapel, giving him his own lunch for sustenance. Tosca jealously insists that she heard voices before entering and, gently rebuffing the artist's amorous advances, lays flowers at the feet of the Madonna and prays. She reminds him of their romantic assignation that evening, but the artist seems distracted. Tosca's mood downturns when she recognises the female visitor in the portrait, although Cavaradossi gently reassures her that she, Tosca, is his one and only love.

Once Tosca has departed Angelotti re-emerges. Cavaradossi gives him the key to his house and suggests hiding in an ancient passageway leading from a well to a hidden vault; there he will be safe from the gaze of evil Baron Scarpia, chief of police. Cannon shots are heard announcing a prisoner's escape, and both men exit at speed. The Sacristan brings news that Napoleon has been defeated and that a *Te Deum* is to be sung in celebration that evening at the Farnese Palace with Floria Tosca. That means double pay for the assembled choirboys, but the mood of celebration is then silenced by the appearance of Scarpia himself. The chapel where Angelotti had hidden is searched: a fan left by his sister to help with his disguise is found, as is Cavaradossi's empty lunch basket. Recognising Angelotti's sister in the portrait, Scarpia concludes that Cavaradossi is in league with the escaped criminal, and resolves to take Cavaradossi's Tosca for himself.

Tosca returns briefly to tell the painter that because of the *Te Deum* she won't be able to meet that evening, only to be confronted by Scarpia, who draws her attention to the fan. Now convinced that Cavaradossi is having an affair, she breaks down in tears and runs off to find him. Scarpia orders his agent Spoletta to follow her and report back to him later that evening. As the sounds of the *Te Deum* begin to envelop the stage, Scarpia menacingly boasts that he has the power to send Cavaradossi to the gallows and keep Tosca for himself.

Act II: Later that same evening, in Scarpia's apartments in the Farnese Palace. The baron sits eating pensively, hoping to hear of Angelotti's and Cavaradossi's capture. He arranges for Tosca to receive a letter upon her arrival, while Spoletta brings news that he followed Tosca to the painter's villa, and although there was no sign of Angelotti they have Cavaradossi in custody. As Tosca, oblivious to Scarpia's plans, sings in a room on the floor below, the scheming chief of police questions Cavaradossi as to Angelotti's whereabouts – to no avail. Tosca bursts in brandishing the letter and, seeing her beloved incarcerated, rushes over and embraces him. He whispers to her not to tell Scarpia anything.

Cavaradossi is bundled into the room next door and tortured while Scarpia tries to find out Angelotti's location from Tosca. At first she stands firm, obeying her lover's wishes, but as his cries of anguish ring out from the room beyond she relents and gives Scarpia the information he requires. Spoletta is despatched to capture Angelotti while Cavaradossi is brought back in, having been badly beaten by Scarpia's henchmen. Desperate that Cavaradossi should not think he has endured such pain in vain, Tosca reassures him that she has said nothing. They hear news that Napoleon's armies were in fact victorious at Marengo, and Cavaradossi cheers. In a fit of pique Scarpia orders the painter's execution.

Tosca asks Scarpia to name his price for saving Cavaradossi, but he is only interested in Tosca herself. Repulsed and confused, Tosca vents her feelings in the aria 'Vissi d'arte'. News is brought that Angelotti committed suicide before Scarpia's men could capture him, which leaves Tosca as the only person who can save Cavaradossi. She accedes to Scarpia's demands and in return Scarpia tells Spoletta to change the execution to a firing squad and simulate the execution 'as in the case of Palmieri', said with emphasis. Tosca assumes that she has saved Cavaradossi, so she now has to fulfil her part of the bargain. She asks that she tell the painter herself, and that Scarpia will then guarantee them both safe passage out of Rome. As he writes the note, Tosca notices on the table the knife with which Scarpia has been peeling an apple. Hiding the knife behind her, when Scarpia moves to embrace her she swings it round and stabs him through the heart. Taking the note from his hand, she places lighted candles on either side of his body, and a crucifix on his chest, before silently departing.

Act III: The scene of Cavaradossi's execution on a platform of the Sant'Angelo Castle. It is just before dawn and the painter is granted one final request – to write a letter. He soon finds himself lost in reverie, and staring aloft at the stars sings 'E lucevan le stelle'. Just as he thinks all is lost Tosca arrives on the scene with Scarpia's note guaranteeing safe conduct. In great excitement, she tells Cavaradossi of Scarpia's grisly end and the events surrounding it, including the planned fake execution. She instructs him how to die convincingly and to lie perfectly still until she calls for him. There is new hope in the air as they run through the plan. The firing party arrives, the execution takes place, a cloth is thrown over the painter's face, and as the soldiers exit Tosca calls upon her beloved to get up as it is now safe. To her horror she discovers that Scarpia had intended to kill him all along – her beloved Cavaradossi lies dead at her feet. Suddenly, all hell is let loose; Scarpia's body has been discovered and in the confusion that follows the soldiers attempt to arrest Tosca, but she tears herself away from the throng and hurls herself off the battlements.

is extremely tense. Tosca's scene with Scarpia has a curiously unsettling changeability about it, one moment threatening, the next soothing. The audience is still not quite sure what to make of this man until in the final section, following his 'Tre sbirri', he tightens the net, his voice bellowing over the *Te Deum* with which he ultimately joins: we are left in no doubt of Scarpia's personality and intentions when he cries, 'Tosca, mi fai dimenticare Iddio!' ('Tosca, you make me forget God!').

The textural choppiness of the opening act spills over into the second. Musical elements do not so much flow effortlessly by, as are thrust up one against the other. Puccini feels less musically certain and distinctive regarding Scarpia. On the one hand he appears to evoke the insidiousness of *verismo* melodrama, on the other the kind of menace typified by Verdi that had never felt entirely convincing in the younger composer's hands. The first unmistakably Puccinian moment of the second act occurs a full five minutes in when the flutes offer a haunting theme which becomes associated with Cavaradossi's plight. As the latter undergoes his initial interrogation, the music – refusing to relax – reflects the changes in Scarpia's technique from fatherly persuasion to unguarded malevolence. This is Puccini at his most cinematographic – one can almost sense him sitting there with a stopwatch, timing each mood and textural change with split-second precision.

With Tosca's arrival and Cavaradossi's incarceration in an adjacent room, the music begins to glide by more easily – momentarily settling before Puccini begins to pile on the emotional pressure. Cavaradossi's cries of pain and Scarpia's malevolence eventually explode in Tosca's agonised relenting. Yet for all this scene's dramatic clout, one cannot help but feel that Puccini was no more comfortable with it than was his audience – for entirely different reasons. The hand at work here seems overtly manipulative, and curiously unengaged. But Puccini's lyrical skill is briefly glimpsed in the magical overlapping phrases shared by Cavaradossi and Tosca following the torture of the painter. It is telling that for all the nerve-shattering events of this act, this is the one moment that Puccini seems genuinely to be living through.

With Cavaradossi's cries of victory at the news of Napoleon's success the music becomes a none-too-distinguished Verdian march. It has been a multi-faceted collage of musical events, but now the music begins to become more expansive as Scarpia attempts to reveal his 'human' side. Tosca responds with her famous 'Vissi d'arte' ('I lived for art'), an aria of modal harmonic luxuriance, which, for all its overwhelming intensity, feels strangely out of place here. Following the hysteria that erupts with Tosca's grisly knifing of her captor, the act ends quietly as though musically exhausted by all that has passed.

CD 2 ④

The launch of the third act by four horns in unison is followed by a dreamy passage strikingly reminiscent of the opening of Act III of *La Bohème*, the modal writing here blending perfectly with the young shepherd boy's folksong as the sun rises. Then the music turns darker, not gradually but in an instant as the strings anticipate Cavaradossi's 'E lucevan le stelle' ('And the stars were shining'): he is attempting to write a letter but is distracted by thoughts of what is to come. Despite the aria's unassailable popularity, it lacks the unforced, natural lyricism of Puccini's finest arias, and is not without its moments of sobbing *verismo* hysteria.

CD 2 ⑤

By contrast, Cavaradossi's 'O dolci mani' is one of the opera's most genuinely moving sections. The ending then swiftly gathers up the various threads as events come thick and fast – a pace that virtually sends us hurtling over the battlements with Tosca. It's a shocking climax to a brutal story, yet revealingly it is the events themselves that tend to shock as much as the fate of those involved. Like many a movie blockbuster, it leaves us feeling as though we've had our money's worth yet, despite the gaudy excess of it all pinning us to our seats, our lives have barely changed.

Before embarking on *Tosca*, Puccini had been warned that it was a drama for which music was, in a sense, barely necessary. This was a challenge that he couldn't resist. The result is an experiment that he was never to repeat, a setting made occasionally impersonal by the techniques he employs, notably in Act II, where the requirement to condense the content of a range of scenes from Sardou's original play produces a succession of rapid episodes, each of which, on their own, might suggest more extended treatment in a different kind of opera: Cavaradossi's interrogation and torture, the deal with Tosca, the attempted rape and murder. The consequence is a brittle world of cinematographic brilliance in which Puccini's lyrical self is for the most part constrained. *Tosca* is the most Wagnerian of Puccini's operas in the sense that the use of motifs to depict characters, ideas and things is strongly apparent. But more than that, the music occasionally supplies us with the characters' unexpressed thoughts, as when Scarpia questions Cavaradossi about Angelotti's whereabouts: although Cavaradossi refuses to say, an orchestral motif tells us he's thinking about the well in which the fugitive is concealed.

Strongly sung and acted with complete conviction, *Tosca* can make an overwhelming impact. Puccini's structural pacing and emotional timing are, at least in the first two acts, exemplary. Despite the ingenuity and virtuosity in the construction, however, *Tosca*'s amplification of emotions and dramatic situations appears rarely warmed by genuine human emotion.

Chapter 7

To the East:
Madama Butterfly

To the East: *Madama Butterfly*

As *Tosca* was staged around the globe, thrilling audiences and dismaying critics in roughly equal proportions, one thought was uppermost in Puccini's mind: what to do next. The solution had been fermenting in his mind for some time, but was yet to take a definitive form.

Europe's incurable fascination with the Orient can be dated back to at least as far as the 1850s, but, as the new century approached, people's appetites for this mysterious and still relatively unknown region sharpened considerably. Nowhere was this more strongly expressed than in the arts. Pottery, paintings, murals, sculpture, fashion, architecture, literature and calligraphy of both Japanese and Chinese origin were all the rage.

Musically the impact of the Far East was most strongly felt in France, especially in the music of Debussy ('Pagodes' from the solo piano *Estampes* of 1903, for example) and Ravel, whose 'Laideronnette, impératrice des pagodes' from his enchanting ballet *Ma Mère l'oye* ('Mother Goose') became a musical blueprint for bustling young ladies, talking nineteen to the dozen behind a blur of shimmering, hand-held fans. Pentatonic scales and passages of rule-breaking parallel 4ths and 5ths became the order of the day – techniques that Puccini had already embraced in the strictly non-oriental context of *La Bohème*'s third act.

What appears to have persuaded Puccini to look to the East for inspiration was a production of David Belasco's new one-act play *Madame Butterfly*, which the composer saw in London in June 1900 while supervising the Covent Garden premiere of *Tosca*. The play's captivating scenario (based on a story by John Luther Long) of an American naval officer marrying a geisha, having a child by her and then returning to America to take himself a 'real' wife was taking the West End by storm. Although Puccini's poor grasp of English meant that he had only caught the general gist of what was being said, he recognised in the play's domestic tragedy an ideal subject for his next opera. Belasco, one of the great theatrical maestros of his day, was a master of passages in which the actors wouldn't utter a word but the audience would be left in no doubt as to what was going on – clearly he was a man after Puccini's own heart.

During the early months of 1900, between various productions of *Tosca*, Puccini was preoccupied with rebuilding his villa in Torre del Lago. It had been in need of serious renovation since he first rented it, but now, as its proud owner, Puccini elected simply to start over again, enlarging the garden area and building an imposing new driveway. However, it was the natural scenery that continued to captivate him. In a letter of July 1900 he describes it as the 'ultimate in contentment, a paradise, Eden'. He even positioned the villa so that 'the extraordinary sunsets could illuminate the surrounding hills on the far side of the lake reflected in its still waters'. Yet the wildlife was viewed as little more than appetising targets: 'deer, boar, hares, rabbits, pheasants, woodcocks and blackbirds' were singled out for special mention, as were 'finches and swallows'.

The villa was ready by the summer and the Puccinis wasted no time in moving in. Giacomo was delighted: Torre del Lago represented for him the ideal retreat away from all the madness of being an idolised celebrity – 'a refuge for the spirit, kingdom, 120 inhabitants, 12 houses. A peaceful place with scrubland running down to the sea.' What he failed to consider, however, was that while he was off gallivanting around Europe, Elvira was often left at home with very little to do. A city girl at heart, she ached for the buzz and excitement of Milan. Additionally, even when Giacomo returned home she felt she was very much last in the queue after his country companions and never-ending stream of visiting friends and business colleagues. She often wrote of her frustrations in letters, but for the time being Puccini carried on regardless.

The end of the year brought him back to earth with a jolt. A production of *La Bohème* at La Scala featuring an ailing Enrico Caruso as Rodolfo and an unsympathetic Mimì (Emma Carelli) was met with stony silence, despite having Toscanini at the helm. This was particularly bad timing as Illica was once again despairing of Puccini's apparent lack of commitment and interest, now in *Madama Butterfly*. Composing was supposed to be Puccini's trade and passion, yet an entire year had flown by without a note being committed to paper.

Fortunately for the composer an immediate distraction was caused by the sudden death of Verdi on 17 January 1901, which threw the entire Italian nation into a state of mourning. Verdi had become a national hero. At a time when a wave of nationalism had created a series of political flashpoints across western Europe, Verdi's music seemed to embody the very essence of Italian culture. His name had even been adopted by the proletariat as a symbol of Italian independence: by way of an ingenious acronym, V.E.R.D.I. was widely understood as *Vittorio Emanuele, Re D'Italia* ('Vittorio Emanuele, King of Italy'), hence the popular cry: 'Viva Verdi!' The death of this iconic figure left the nation bereft.

Just as everyone was beginning to come to terms with Verdi's passing, Puccini received news that David Belasco had granted him the rights to turn *Madame Butterfly* into an opera. Illica was at last free to begin drawing up a scenario, although at this stage Ricordi had severe reservations about the whole enterprise. By September Illica had produced a detailed three-act breakdown of the main plot which earned general approval. Act I would be set entirely in Japan, focusing on the courtship and marriage of Pinkerton and Butterfly; Act II would then

be split into two scenes designed to emphasise the cultural differences between the Americans and the Japanese (the first set in Butterfly's home, the second in the American Consulate). All of Act III was to take place back in Butterfly's home.

Giuseppe Verdi in 1886 by Giovanni Boldini

Puccini meanwhile had been busy researching authentic Japanese music with a view to adapting some melodies in the score. However, his greatest enthusiasm was reserved for his newest and most prized possession: his first motor car, a De Dion Bouton. Puccini had caught the driving bug from Franchetti, who as President of the Italian Automobile Club already owned a Renault and a Mercedes. Like Rachmaninov, Puccini fell in love with the exhilaration and romance of motoring at high speed. The difference, though, was that Rachmaninov was able to cut his teeth speeding around his huge estate in Russia, whereas Puccini took immediately to the open road, not always with the greatest care or expertise.

Puccini's attention was also taken up with a more serious domestic matter. Never the most faithful of men, he succeeded for the most part in keeping his dalliances away from Elvira's piercing gaze. She was not the kind of woman to sit back and turn a blind eye to his activities, although he usually managed to bluff his way out of any trouble if it arose. However, by the summer of 1901 his ongoing relationship with a young woman from Turin called Corinna was proving decidedly uncomfortable. Puccini is likely to have come across her when supervising rehearsals for the Turin premiere of *Tosca*.

Puccini's little trips to Milan, Pisa and elsewhere to meet Corinna may not have gone unobserved, but the crunch came when Elvira gained possession of a letter that left no doubt as to what had been going on. Although Puccini promised to finish it there and then, it would in fact be 1903 before the affair finally came to an end. Puccini had no real excuse for his behaviour, but – as he saw it – Elvira seemed old before her time, she constantly put herself at odds with the kind of life he wanted, and legally she was still married to someone else. Corinna was young, attractive, vibrant and unattached: everything, in fact, that Elvira wasn't.

Puccini's relationship with Elvira became even more strained the following year when her daughter, Fosca, who had continued to live with them since their elopement, married and left home. She had acted as an emotional buffer zone in the Puccini household, and her departure had far more impact than either Elvira or Puccini had imagined, as he wrote in no uncertain terms to Fosca in two letters dated August 1902.

Meanwhile, Puccini had managed to complete the first act of *Madama Butterfly* and was about to start work on the second when he dropped a bombshell: he wanted the consulate scene removed and the first part of Act II welded together with Act III to create a new two-act structure, with the second being in two clearly defined parts. Illica seems to have come round to Puccini's way of thinking quite quickly but Giacosa had to be talked into making all the necessary changes, having initially resigned in a fit of pique. (Following the premiere, Puccini would go on to revise the work three times between 1904 and 1907, to the extent that there is no completely definitive version of *Butterfly*. But despite the cuts that Puccini variously sanctioned along the way, the work's essential dramatic outlines remained the same.)

1903 didn't get off to the happiest of starts. Giacosa was still smarting over Puccini's decision to jettison the consulate scene and Elvira was behaving coolly following the revelations concerning Corinna. However, it was the close proximity of two otherwise unconnected events that was to change the course of the composer's personal life irrevocably.

Puccini was never the safest of drivers. He was far more drawn to the bracing power of speed and risk-taking than simply getting to a destination in one piece. During the previous year he had managed to slide off the road into a ditch near Lucca, fortunately inflicting only a few slight scratches and bruises on himself and his passenger. But on 25 February 1903, when he was returning home late in foggy conditions with Elvira and Tonio after dining in Lucca, his chauffeur took a bend too fast, left the road, shot down an embankment and turned the car over. Elvira, Tonio and the driver were thrown clear, and although mother and son were not much more than badly shaken, the chauffeur had broken his thigh bone. Of Puccini there was no sign. Fortunately a doctor who lived nearby had heard the accident and came to see what had happened. Puccini was eventually found lying in a burrow underneath the upturned car, unable to speak at first due to shock and with his shin broken. He would walk with a slight limp for the rest of his life.

The weeks and months of painful recovery, during which Puccini discovered that he may be diabetic, were marked by a constant stream of telegrams and get-well wishes from a host of friends and dignitaries, and even the King of Italy. A letter to Ricordi dated 29 August shows the composer on the road to recovery:

> *I am fat and flourishing again. As far as my leg is concerned, I am getting on not so badly but walking with great difficulty and still with two sticks. My general health is very good. There are two professors here, Ciamician, a distinguished chemist, and Napini, the principal of the University of Bologna, also a chemist, who have subjected my urine to infallible tests and have found no trace of glucose, with the result that I am eating the hotel food, including the sweets.*

Some of those close to Puccini were not quite so forgiving, most notably Ricordi. The publisher saw the accident as a form of retribution for Puccini's clandestine affair with Corinna, whom he considered little better than a harlot. He even went so far as to suggest that Puccini's ill-health was the result of a syphilitic infection he had picked up from the girl. Puccini felt well and truly chastised, and from then on his days with Corinna were numbered. In the meantime he spent nearly six months 'coaching' a stunning young Japanese soprano in the central role of *Madama Butterfly*, much to Elvira's chagrin.

Yet the deciding factor in the break-up of the Corinna affair was an event that occurred the day after the crash: Elvira's husband died, so she was finally free to marry Puccini. At first the composer was resistant. He clearly adored Corinna: he even managed to see her again, and there was talk of an elopement to Switzerland. However, under pressure from friends and relatives, Puccini was forced to enter into a legal arrangement with Corinna announcing that he was to marry Elvira, that the affair was over, and that he would pay her a substantial sum by way of compensation. On 4 January 1904 Puccini and Elvira were married in the parish church of Torre del Lago in the utmost privacy. Momentary respite was provided by the arrival of Puccini's first motor boat.

Despite suffering constant pain from his injuries and coping with his churning emotions following the break-up of his relationship with Corinna, Puccini had somehow managed to keep his creative flame burning throughout the year – to the extent that just four days after the wedding ceremony, on 17 February rehearsals started for the La Scala premiere of *Madama Butterfly*. The first-rate cast included Rosina Storchio (Butterfly), Giovanni Zenatello (Pinkerton) and Giuseppe De Luca (Sharpless); the conductor was the well-known Cleofonte Campanini and no expense had been spared on the production. Everyone was convinced that Puccini had produced a hit.

Rosina Storchio as Butterfly

What followed, however, was one of the most humiliating public maulings a composer of international repute has ever received. Many passages were drowned out with jeers, whistles and catcalls, including the love duet in Act I; and when the kimono of the rather stoutly built Butterfly unexpectedly billowed up (the singer was Toscanini's mistress) there were delighted cries of 'pregnant' from the stalls. The moment the dawn breaks before the final scene was accompanied by farmyard noises, while other numbers, including 'Un bel dì', were greeted with silence. The whole thing had been organised by Puccini's musical enemies, most probably whipped up by Ricordi's infamous publishing rival Sonzogno, who was going through something of a lean spell. The papers gave sensationalised coverage, and one can hardly blame them: such uproar was manna from heaven for a reporter. There were also accusations of plagiarism – of his own music, and that of other composers.

Puccini immediately withdrew *Madama Butterfly*, writing to a friend:

> *I am still shocked by all that has happened – not so much for what they did to my poor Butterfly, but for all the poison they spat on me as an artist and as a man... They have printed all kinds of things! That first performance was a Dantean Inferno, prepared in advance.*

Within days Puccini was hard at work making changes and cuts for an intended second performance in Brescia on 24 May (all other performances were put on hold). This was now a damage-limitation exercise, for everything depended on how the opera would be received the second time. In the event no one need have worried, and Puccini's absolute faith in his latest masterwork was vindicated. Puccini was still a big draw at the box office and there was nothing his detractors could do about it. (In 1908 alone *Tosca* would be heard in fifty-three French opera houses, twelve in Spain, eight in both Austria and Germany, and three in Switzerland. *La Bohème* was more popular still, while *Butterfly* was performed in twenty-four European cities. Tellingly, though, it was only after Puccini's death that it finally returned to Milan.)

In contrast to the occasionally shocking brutality of *Tosca*, *Madama Butterfly* is a work of exquisite sophistication. The opening act's dramatic and emotional pacing bears an unmistakable similarity to that of *La Bohème*, innocent exuberance being transformed into the music of love. Yet whereas Mimì becomes musically absorbed into the action from her first utterance – she and Rodolfo sing as one from their initial encounter – Puccini musically symbolises the cultural divide between Pinkerton and Butterfly (there is a distinct change in atmosphere when she first appears) so that their passion for each other becomes an act of stylistic unification. On a practical level, as well as equipping the orchestra with an enlarged percussion section, Puccini uses two techniques to infuse the score with oriental exoticism: he imports Japanese tunes and incorporates them in the harmony (his biographer Mosco Carner has identified seven), and he invents tunes in the Japanese style, using intervals and rhythms which the audience would 'hear' as Japanese. While the worlds of Butterfly and Pinkerton are clearly delineated, Butterfly, who has crossed over culturally, is often clothed in 'western' music, giving her common cause with other Puccini heroines.

The opera opens not with an outburst of lurid exotica but a fugal sequence based on a snappy little motif suggestive of the hustle and bustle of geishas. It's an ingenious idea which is insinuated into the musical textures with bracing freedom, forming a contrast with Pinkerton's laid-back cantabile. The opening of *The Star-Spangled Banner*, announced on brass and woodwind, is immediately counterpointed by a melodic variant in the form of Pinkerton's credo, in which he announces, 'The Yankee drops anchor for random adventure, and life is not worth living until he makes the flowers of every region his treasure'. In just a few words we are right

Madama Butterfly

Act I: Lieutenant B.F. Pinkerton of the United States Navy inspects the Nagasaki hillside house he has just leased from Goro the marriage broker, who has also secured him a geisha wife, Cio-Cio-San (known to her friends as 'Butterfly'), and three servants, including Butterfly's faithful Suzuki. Sharpless, the American Consul at Nagasaki, arrives out of breath from the climb. It quickly becomes obvious that Sharpless disapproves of the match, for while Pinkerton is in a position to take it or leave it, strict Japanese social etiquette dictates that for Butterfly the marriage is of enormous significance. Pinkerton laughs off his concerns while extolling the carefree life of an American sailor, and raises his glass to his betrothed, Kate, in America.

The two Americans are distracted from their conversation by the distant singing of Butterfly, who arrives with some friends. Sharpless's concerns about Pinkerton are heightened as he learns that this is no ordinary Japanese arranged marriage – Butterfly has fallen very much in love and as a result has secretly renounced her religious beliefs, intending to embrace Pinkerton's Christian faith. She has, in effect, cut herself off from her friends and family and is now dependent on him for everything. The officials arrive and the Imperial Commissioner performs the service with all due ceremony. As the guests drink a toast in celebration of the newly wed couple, there is a disturbance and Butterfly's uncle, the Bonze (a Buddhist monk), bursts in. He has discovered his niece's renunciation of her faith and calls upon her relatives to denounce her publicly. Angry at the interruption, Pinkerton clears the house, dries Butterfly's tears and the pair sing of their love for each other in an extended duet.

Act II, Part 1: Three years have passed. Pinkerton has left promising to return 'when the robins nest', yet there is still no sign of him. Every day Butterfly waits patiently for her husband's return, staring out across the harbour for any sign of his vessel. She sings the opera's most famous aria 'Un bel dì, vedremo'. Sharpless enters carrying a letter from Pinkerton which explains he is now married to an American and that she will be joining him in Nagasaki. On seeing the note in his hand, Butterfly is so overcome with emotion that she fails to grasp the crushing significance of its contents and assumes that he is returning to her at last. As Sharpless attempts to explain the real situation, Goro appears on the scene accompanied by a wealthy suitor for Butterfly's affections: Prince Yamadori. Even though the meagre funds Pinkerton left have nearly run out, she dismisses all possibility of remarrying, insisting that Pinkerton would never desert her.

Sharpless tries again to make Butterfly see sense, but she merely responds by producing the baby boy Dolore ('Trouble') to whom she has given birth since Pinkerton's departure; she is certain that this will bring the sailor back to her. She ultimately silences Sharpless by pointing out that if Pinkerton had jilted her, she would have only two choices: either to return to her former life as a geisha or to die, and she doesn't see the former as a real option. Just as it seems as though the situation might overwhelm her, the sound of cannon fire rings out: the *Abraham Lincoln* has returned with Pinkerton on board. Utterly convinced that she was right after all, Butterfly, helped by Suzuki, decorates the house with fresh blossom and the two settle down for the night waiting for a hero's return.

Act II, Part 2: As the sun rises Butterfly sings a lullaby to her child, whom she takes into another room. Suzuki is left to welcome Sharpless and Pinkerton, and is on the point of giving her mistress the wonderful news of Pinkerton's arrival when the full implication of Kate's presence (she has come with them) hits home. Pinkerton is overwhelmed to discover that Butterfly has kept a vigil awaiting his return all this time and is so filled with remorse for his heartless actions that he rushes out, leaving Sharpless to sort everything out.

Butterfly has meanwhile heard all the commotion and rushes in expecting to find her beloved, only to discover the truth of the situation. There is no hysteria. Instead she nobly bears the full brunt of the news, wishing Kate every happiness and promising that if Pinkerton would care to drop by in half an hour he may collect his son. She then dismisses Suzuki and takes out the dagger with which her father had committed suicide. Bowing before a statue of the Buddha she resolves that it is better to die with honour than live in shame. Suzuki ushers in the little boy, whom Butterfly cuddles one last time before sending him into the garden to play. As Pinkerton returns to pick up his son, she stabs herself to death.

at the heart of Pinkerton's personality and Puccini is careful to provide him with music of great beauty, as if to make the point that he is not in himself a bad person – it is his effect on others and the consequences of his thoughtless actions that are so terrible. The parallels with Puccini's own personality could hardly be more pointedly drawn.

Butterfly and her entourage approach from the distance to the sound of the first of the traditional Japanese melodies that Puccini employs in the opera – a Kabuki theatre melody known as 'The Lion of Enchigo'. There follows a magical episode littered with oriental whole-tone colourings, sung by Butterfly with female chorus; typically she is heard before being seen. Throughout the opera, most notably at the climax of the first act's concluding love duet, this music is associated with Butterfly's intense feelings for Pinkerton.

The wedding scene features a snatch of the Japanese national anthem and a phrase from the folksong *The High Mountain*. Here the music of the two cultures overlaps and entwines with glowing anticipation of what is to come. The dramatic appearance of the Bonze is laced with exotic, Eastern whole tones and serves to underline the seriousness of what Butterfly is undertaking. The act ends with Puccini's longest and finest love duet ('Bimba, dagli occhi' / 'Vogliatemi bene'), in which Pinkerton and Butterfly shut out any doubts and anxieties with music of transcendental radiance.

CD 2 ⑥-⑦

If the first act is all about duality expressed in a single symphonic sweep, the second is almost monothematic in terms of its claustrophobic concentration on Butterfly's plight. Revealingly, Act I contains not a single traditional aria, something for which Puccini soon makes amends in the second act, with Butterfly's 'Un bel dì, vedremo' ('One fine day he'll come back'). This popular number may appear to be little more than another of Puccini's heart-stopping outpourings

CD 2 ⑧

of golden melody, yet closer inspection reveals its subtle progression from calm confidence to stoic belief, the delusory nature of which is revealed by the music's sense of despair.

The scene in which Sharpless attempts to confront Butterfly with the truth of Pinkerton's infidelity is one of the most extended examples of Puccini's conversational style. The action itself is almost static, yet the collage of musical events gives the strange sensation of things moving quickly. Snippets of ideas course continually through the music, giving the attentive listener a series of dramatic cues. The changes of mood, as unsettling as anything in *Tosca*, are achieved with great subtlety.

From the gentle waltz that accompanies Butterfly serving tea there is a seamless musical transition into her dramatic, defiant cries in response to Sharpless's forebodings. Butterfly retains her dignity to the last, yet it is not her words but the music that reveals the full extent of her feelings. Our harrowing emotional journey continues as one minute we are thrown into despair by the hapless Butterfly's tragic situation, then we are soothed by the wordless Humming Chorus that concludes the first section.

CD 2 [9]

The second part of Act II opens with a five-minute intermezzo, which initially returns to the gloomy chromaticisms of *Tosca* before building up a head of steam. There follows the magical depiction of morning – complete with birdsong – that had inspired the outbreak of farmyard noises at the work's La Scala premiere. Then, after a trio for Suzuki and the two Americans, Pinkerton sings his one great, heart-stopping aria 'Addio, fiorito asil' ('Farewell, flower-decked sanctuary').

The scene with Kate, in which the truth finally dawns on Butterfly, forms a profound contrast, with its chamber-scale, Debussyan orchestration. This is where Puccini plays his masterstroke. Unlike Mimì and Tosca, Butterfly undergoes a colossal change; during her long wait for Pinkerton she has grown from an innocent geisha full of girlish devotion to a tragic figure of moving nobility. Her suicide is a moment of overwhelming dignity as well as tragedy. If we weep for Mimì and sit slack-jawed at Tosca's shocking exit, for Butterfly's demise our reactions are far more complex. Despite Pinkerton having had some of the loveliest music, one feels a sense of utter revulsion for the American as he blunders in at the eleventh hour, not to seek reconciliation and forgiveness but to commit an act of overwhelming selfishness by collecting 'his' son.

Madama Butterfly is the last in a trilogy of operas that continue to play to packed houses around the world. It may lack La Bohème's formal perfection and constant stream of invention, or the sheer visceral clout of Tosca, yet for today's audiences it is the most popular of all. It is not hard to fathom why. The emotional journey along which Butterfly travels outpaces anything else in the Puccini canon, and the more expansive scale of the piece makes it possible for Puccini to explore in greater depth the implications of Pinkerton's actions as they begin to unravel in the second act. Most of all, music and storyline are integrated with a naturalism that occasionally eludes the opera's predecessors.

Interestingly, America would also play a large part in Puccini's next opera – but in a different place and time.

Chapter 8

To the West:
La fanciulla del West

> "I can see him now, strolling up and
> down the Promenade des Anglais
> in that leisurely manner that was so
> characteristic of him; indeed, so slow
> was his progress that it could hardly
> be called walking at all, for every few
> yards he would come to a complete
> standstill, pausing to light one of his
> eternal cigarettes, or to think over
> some point in the conversation that
> interested or amused him..."

To the West: *La fanciulla del West*

Giulio Ricordi, Puccini's long-suffering publisher, never really understood the appeal of *Madama Butterfly*. For him it was little more than a sophisticated weepy, a work that – while exquisitely polished in itself – did not remotely show what Puccini was capable of. Ricordi's obvious disappointment over *Butterfly* hurt Puccini more than perhaps he was prepared to admit. The result was a renewed determination to find something for his next operatic project that would give Ricordi the novelty he so obviously craved.

Of the subjects Illica initially suggested, the only one that seems to have got at least as far as the drawing board was Victor Hugo's *Notre Dame de Paris*. Puccini, however, felt he had come up with an even better idea: three one-act operas based on the gloomy short stories of the Russian author and political activist Maxim Gorky (1868–1936). All looked set fair this time until Ricordi pointed out the cost involved in putting on three different works in one evening, let alone the difficulties of attracting audiences to such a venture.

Puccini had meanwhile been secretly in contact with Valentino Soldani, a Tuscan playwright who was making an operatic adaptation of his successful stage play *Margherita da Cortona* (about a courtesan's conversion to Christianity and entry into sainthood). This quickly came to nothing as did at least two other subjects sent to Puccini for his approval by the distinguished Italian playwright and future mentor of Mussolini, Gabriele d'Annunzio (1863–1938). Next to enter the frame, at Illica's suggestion, was *Maria Antonietta*; Puccini had already turned this idea down in 1901, and it was soon to be abandoned again. Illica then suggested *Ramuntcho* by Pierre Loti, a thoroughly unworkable tale of a military man who returns home after three years in the wars to discover that his sweetheart has taken holy orders.

During this period Puccini produced only two new pieces. The 1904 song *Canto d'anime*, a march-like setting of words by Illica, is of no great interest, and was composed by way of payment for a large number of gramophone recordings that Puccini had been allowed to select from the Gramophone and Typewriter Company catalogue. In January 1905 he produced a Requiem for three-part chorus, viola and harmonium, written to commemorate the fourth anniversary of Verdi's death, in conjunction with the opening of a new concert hall in the Milan Conservatoire bearing Verdi's name. Behind the grand title, however, lies a hushed, five-and-a-half-minute setting that Puccini appears to have composed in a hurry and to which he never returned.

During a trip to England for the London premiere of *Madama Butterfly* in July, Puccini renewed his acquaintance with a lady he had first met the previous year. Sybil Seligman, intelligent and glamorous, and the wife of a London banker, was to enter into a remarkable correspondence with Puccini which lasted until the end of the composer's life. He sent her more than 700 letters. It seems that there was a brief affair, but in order to prevent scandal on both sides it was decided to keep the relationship platonic. She was a remarkable woman in many ways, one who understood and empathised with Puccini the man and the artist in a way that Elvira never did. She even began making helpful, or at least well-intentioned, suggestions of subjects for possible operatic treatment: Rudyard Kipling's *The Light that Failed* was one, Tolstoy's *Anna Karenina* another.

In the early spring of 1906 Puccini travelled with Elvira to Nice to see a performance of *Manon Lescaut*. Here they bumped into Sybil Seligman's family, an occasion remembered by Sybil's son Vincent. In 1938 Vincent published his various observations in *Puccini Among Friends*, an invaluable collection that illuminates aspects of Puccini's personality not always on show to his business colleagues:

> *I can see him now, strolling up and down the Promenade des Anglais in that leisurely manner that was so characteristic of him; indeed, so slow was his progress that it could hardly be called walking at all, for every few yards he would come to a complete standstill, pausing to light one of his eternal cigarettes, or to think over some point in the conversation that interested or amused him... He took considerable care of his personal appearance and was invariably well dressed, although – unlike many other musicians – he avoided sartorial eccentricities or exaggerations... More clearly than anything else I remember the look of indulgent affection in his large brown eyes, and the rare sweetness of his frank smile – and yet, even when he was in his happiest and jolliest mood, there always seemed to lurk at the corners of his mouth a hint of melancholy, if not of actual suffering – the look that one sometimes sees on the faces of the blind.*

One can imagine how Puccini's 'large brown eyes' and his irascible loveability must have saved him on countless occasions when his collaborators were sorely frustrated by his tendency to put the other pleasures of life before composing.

Elvira – or 'my policeman' as Puccini referred to her in social circles – formed a stark contrast to her husband's warmth and charm. Vincent Seligman thought her 'a handsome woman' despite her 'very large hands and feet', but found her uncertain temper and overbearing personality threatening to the point that even delivering a polite kiss on the cheek involved quite a force of will on his part.

Meanwhile, in finding the right opera subject, it was back to D'Annunzio, who on the basis of a series of favourable meetings in early 1906 was enthusiastically brought on board and asked to produce a story outline of his own devising. The poet proposed stories like *La rosa di Cipra* and *La Parisina*, but Puccini found the overheated prose too garish and declined the collaboration. 'I don't want a realism of the kind you would find hard to accept,' he wrote unequivocally to D'Annunzio, 'but a "quid medium" that captivates the listeners through dolorous and amorous action, which logically lives and throbs in a halo of the poetry of life, rather than of dreams.' Meanwhile Ricordi had managed to secure the rights to *La Femme et le pantin* ('The Woman and the Puppet'), a raunchy novel by Pierre Louÿs in which the central character, Conchita, is a sado-masochistic temptress who gives herself to a leering admirer only after he's beaten her up.

Maurice Vaucaire was hired to write the libretto for this as Giacosa was by then fatally ill with asthma (he died at the beginning of September 1906). Contracts were drawn up and the green light given just as Puccini got cold feet about the debauched nature of the central character. In desperation he turned to Sybil in London, who had previously suggested Oscar Wilde's *A Florentine Tragedy* – another story based around a sexually manipulative woman, but with a less sensational storyline (it was in fact taken up by Zemlinsky a decade later). Puccini took it upon himself to commission a French translation from Illica. This was simply too much for Ricordi, however. The constant flow of ideas and costly literary contracts leading to nothing had tried his patience beyond endurance. When he heard about the Wilde idea, in a rage he told Puccini to throw it on the fire.

Puccini was prepared to wait until Ricordi cooled off and so allowed the impasse to remain when he set sail for America on 9 January 1907; a Puccini season in New York was to include the premiere of *Madama Butterfly* on 11 February. Puccini mentioned in a letter to Sybil that although Caruso's singing was 'magnificent', as a person he left a great deal to be desired – 'he won't learn anything, he's lazy and he's too pleased with himself.' Caruso, who was to sing in the premiere of Puccini's next opera, later drew a delightful series of caricatures of the composer.

It was during this visit that Puccini saw three plays by David Belasco: *The Rose of the Rancho*, *The Music Master* and *The Girl of the Golden West*. It was the last of these that aroused his interest, although he had reservations about certain aspects of the plot. He discussed it with Sybil during a visit to London in June and it was arranged to have the play translated into Italian and sent to the composer at Torre del Lago. Puccini was at last truly fired up to begin work. As Illica was by now busy working on other projects, Puccini turned to Carlo Zangarini, a bright young star in the Italian literary firmament who had come highly recommended by Tito Ricordi, Giulio's son.

At first all seemed well – Puccini excitedly reporting to Giulio Ricordi that 'The *Girl* promises to become a second *Bohème*. But more vigorous, more daring, and on an altogether larger scale.' Yet as the months went by Puccini became increasingly exasperated with the slow progress on the libretto, and by April 1908 he had reached the end of his tether. Zangarini was forced to move aside and another Tito recommendation, Guelfo Civinini, was swiftly signed up; to the great relief of all concerned, he hit it off with Puccini immediately. The first two acts were reconfigured to Puccini's satisfaction and on 24 May 1908, nearly four and a half years after the Milan premiere of *Butterfly*, Puccini again put his operatic pen to paper.

All Puccini's creative energies were focused on the libretto of *La fanciulla del West* that Civinini had prepared for him. However, he could work only falteringly on the opera during that summer and autumn. He was constantly distracted by throat problems (probably the first sign of the disease that would ultimately kill him) and the indifferent weather, which kept swinging unpredictably between extremes of temperature. Additionally he was finding the opera difficult to feel his way into, largely because of the cultural void between his own background and the work's subject matter. There were at this point no Westerns, no stirring theme tunes such as *The Magnificent Seven* or *The Big Country*, and, with nothing to fall back on, Puccini had to invent a new genre: the operatic Western. However, this was to prove the least of his problems.

Following Puccini's automobile accident in 1903, Doria Manfredi, the charming sixteen-year-old daughter of a widowed mother, had been taken on to help with his convalescence. Five years later she was still working as a general house-servant at Torre del Lago. For years Elvira had been getting increasingly upset about Puccini's various infidelities, and by the autumn of 1908 she'd finally had enough, and poor Doria found herself scolded by the fury of Elvira's invective. Ironically Puccini was, for once in his life, entirely innocent of any impropriety, but Elvira was baying for blood and would not be denied.

There seems to have been no particular incident that sparked off Elvira's vitriolic outburst, but quickly one thing led to another. Doria was sacked and Elvira immediately set about a vengeful plan to discredit her husband. She put it about the village, their friends and family that Doria was a whore who had wrecked their marriage. She even claimed to have found them in bed together. So plausible were her accusations and so potent her fury that almost everyone believed her – including Doria's family, who, naturally enough, blamed Puccini. It escalated to the newspapers. In January 1909 Puccini, exasperated, informed Elvira that their marriage was over and headed for Rome in an attempt to clear the air. The following day Doria took a draught of poison and after five days of agonising pain passed away on 28 January. The autopsy showed that Doria died a virgin.

Puccini was therefore in the clear as regards Elvira's unfounded accusations, yet the situation refused to go away. Publications around the world were full of stories regarding the Doria affair, especially when the Manfredi family took Elvira to court for causing their daughter's tragic suicide through defamation of character. In July 1909 Elvira was found guilty and sentenced to five months in prison. Puccini intervened and since Doria's family now felt legally vindicated they agreed to a generous out-of-court settlement. The charges were dropped, with Elvira having narrowly avoided jail.

Throughout the entire episode Elvira stuck to her guns and despite the evidence of the autopsy continued to pour bile on her husband and anyone else prepared to speak up in his defence. It was only after the court case that she appears to have come to her senses. By the August of that year the Puccinis were reconciled and Elvira was, by her standards, behaving in a compliant manner. But Puccini never forgave her; haunted by images of the poor servant girl who had become caught up in this tragic domestic squabble, he even considered suicide for a time. Ultimately, however, he recognised that even though Elvira had been wrong on this occasion he had to take some responsibility for fuelling her anxieties and, by extension, for the tragedy of Doria's death.

As a consequence of everything that had happened, and through having lost at least eight months on *La fanciulla del West*, Puccini set to work on the opera with unprecedented single-mindedness and dedication. The short score was completed just three months later during November. January 1910 saw the first act fully scored, Act II followed in April, and on 6 August Puccini signed off the final page. Both he and Toscanini considered it the finest thing he had written so far, and they were fully vindicated by the audience's rapturous welcome at the work's premiere on 10 December 1910 at New York's Metropolitan Opera House.

Arturo Toscanini, c. 1898

With Toscanini conducting a star-studded cast led by Caruso as Dick Johnson and Emmy Destinn as Minnie, the audience was ecstatic. Tickets had changed hands on the black market for as much as $150, a small fortune in those days. The production broke all box-office records and, in a local poll, Puccini was voted 'the most famous man in the world'. He was warmly embraced as a major celebrity and fêted wherever he went. He fell in love with New York's breathless pace of life and all the new gadgets that were then becoming available. One of his most devoted fans, the

inventor Thomas Edison, made him a gift of his most up-to-date gramophone.

Yet typically the critics were less generous. In general they missed Puccini's usual melodic flair and also had difficulty with his 'advanced' orchestral sonorities and harmonies – these included the use of melodies and phrases which moved in whole-tones, and complex chord sequences, some using the tritone (or 'devil's interval'); in fact, Act I of *La fanciulla* ends on a discord. Such techniques were as nothing compared to the music regularly encountered in the concert hall by composers such as Mahler, Strauss and Schoenberg, but were far more complex than was normally associated with Italian opera. Some observers considered *La fanciulla*'s staging to be rather more impressive than the music, while others commented that it merely emphasised the need for some home-grown American opera. Puccini was also attacked in the Italian press – somewhat ironically, considering America's response – for 'conservatism' and 'cosy commercialism'. This was not helped by the general mood of the times, which was becoming increasingly antagonistic towards opera: the genre was viewed by progressives as retrograde and a bastion of tradition. At least they had enjoyed the spectacle of witnessing the only opera in which the composer stipulates the appearance of a real horse on stage!

Until comparatively recently *La fanciulla del West* has lagged behind Puccini's most celebrated offspring in terms of both its popularity and its frequency of performance. Puccini had reinvented himself and was attempting to move with the times, stripping expression to its essentials without recourse to the usual big arias. The results were neither traditional enough for the traditionalists nor modern enough for the modernists; consequently the opera was in a stylistic no man's land. Yet, freed from the constraints of chronology and contemporary artistic taste, *La fanciulla* emerges as arguably Puccini's most individual work since *La Bohème*.

We feel the change from the opening bars, the whole-tone colourings of which have nothing to do with establishing local colour but are as vital a part of the musical language as they were for Debussy and (in a different way) Richard Strauss. There is an occasional, snappily exuberant rhythmic twist, which gives the music a confident swagger unlike anything Puccini had so far produced. The scene that follows, in which the various customers chat among themselves, is the most cheerily carefree music Puccini had penned since the second act of *La Bohème*. One can imagine the composer escaping the emotional agonies of his private life in this alternative world. Snatches from popular songs of the time are woven into the musical fabric, perfectly offset by the gentle nostalgia of Jake Wallace's 'Che faranno' (sung to the melody of the traditional song, *Old Dog Tray*).

Puccini maintains this stream-of-consciousness style throughout the entire first act; the brief lyrical interludes and delightful orchestral asides – an ass braying, the clip-clopping arrival of the pony express – are subsumed into the music's unquenchable onward flow. The closing scene for Minnie, Johnson and Nick achieves a sublime beauty all its own simply by not trying too hard. Indeed, the way in which Puccini encapsulates the lovers' rediscovery of their feelings for one another is far more natural than the full-on ecstasy of Mimì and Rodolfo's first encounter in *La Bohème*. Discernible in this act, among the Puccinian whole-tone harmonies and pentatonic melodies, are perhaps the seeds of both the classic western movie tradition, and the popular American style which would emerge in Aaron Copland's *Appalachian Spring* and *Billy the Kid*.

La fanciulla del West

Act I: The action takes place in a mining camp at the foot of the Cloudy Mountains during the mid-nineteenth-century gold rush. The curtain rises on the interior of a spit-and-sawdust saloon named 'The Polka'. Here miners drink, smoke and gamble under the watchful but affectionate eye of the bar's owner Minnie, the 'Golden Girl' of the opera's title. She's greatly loved and respected by the miners and has even set up a school during the winter months to try to instil a little knowledge and self-respect into the rough-necked bunch. For their part they trust her enough to leave their gold pickings in a barrel behind the bar for safekeeping.

Minnie is protected by two Native American heavies, Billy Jackrabbit and Wowkle (Billy's squaw), while the bar is tended by the popular Nick. Minnie makes her entrance by breaking up the squabbling that has broken out during the opening scene. But it's all essentially good-natured fun and the clientele make it up to Minnie by presenting her with small gifts – ribbons, scarves and such like. Jack Rance, the sheriff, has marrying designs on Minnie, but she doesn't altogether trust the lawman and firmly rebuffs his advances.

A stranger arrives in town, a bandit named Dick Johnson. He orders a whisky and a period of mutual recognition slowly unwinds between him and Minnie. It seems the two briefly met some time ago, fell in love and now seem happy to make up for lost time, much to the annoyance of Rance and the others. Before tempers fray, however, José Castro, a 'greaser' (or plunderer of Californian gold camps) and a member of the notorious Ramerrez gang, is dragged in and promises to lead the miners to the gang's hide-out if they spare his life. In fact he has recognised the stranger 'Johnson' as none other than Ramerrez and surreptitiously informs him that he will lead the miners away from the town while the rest of the gang move in and steal the gold from the saloon. 'Johnson' is left behind with Minnie and the two of them agree to meet up at her place later that evening.

Act II: After a touching domestic scene in Minnie's small abode between her two Native American servants, Minnie enters and dismisses them as she prepares for her guest to arrive. Johnson and Minnie declare their undying love for each other. A blizzard begins to rage outside. Minnie offers to put Johnson up for the night when there is a knock at the door; she conceals him behind some curtains. It transpires that Rance and the miners have discovered the truth about Johnson being Ramerrez. Once they have left, Minnie tackles Johnson who admits he had intended to steal the gold but since falling in love with Minnie wants to mend his ways and reform. He leaves and seconds later a shot rings out. Johnson staggers back in and Minnie hides him again, this time in her loft room above the main living area.

Rance returns and searches the apartment for any sign of Johnson. At first Minnie feigns innocence but then a drop of blood falls on Rance's hand and the game is up. Johnson crawls down from the upstairs room and collapses on the floor. Now desperate to find any way of saving her lover, Minnie suggests they play to see who wins the best of three hands of poker. If she wins she keeps Johnson; if Rance wins he gets his man, with Minnie into the bargain. Rance readily agrees and the game begins. Minnie manages to secrete some high cards about her person and with the score at one deal each she distracts Rance with the ruse that she needs a drink and fixes a deck in her favour. Rance is apoplectic at losing and departs in a huff, leaving Minnie alone again with the man she loves and whose life she has just saved.

Act III: A forest clearing where Rance and the miners are sitting. The hunt is on again for Johnson, who has been forced out of Minnie's house for fear of being rediscovered there. Following a series of false alarms, Johnson is eventually captured and the men resolve to hang him. He is on the point of swinging when Minnie appears on the scene and begs the miners to release him as a personal favour to her, especially as she has done so much for them in the past. Ultimately, and much to Rance's disgust, the miners relent – allowing Minnie and Johnson to walk off hand-in-hand into the sunset to begin a new and better life together.

The second act opens sparklingly with a number of delightful orchestral touches, the little scene with the Native Americans acting as a gentle on-stage curtain-raiser to Minnie's entrance. Puccini relies less heavily on the string section in *La fanciulla*, even if it remains the emotional powerhouse whenever there is a surging emotional eruption. In Minnie's extended scene with Johnson the strings repeatedly, and tantalisingly, sound on the point of launching forth. Throughout this section the orchestra cajoles and comments on, supports, sets up and enhances the action, but rarely imposes itself in the way one expects from Puccini. As in the opening act, he never overheats his material and thereby avoids it sounding remotely *verismo*. He continually adjusts the musical focus, one minute bringing the orchestra to the fore, then easing off to the point that it provides little more than atmospheric background music to accompany the action on stage.

The final and shortest act exchanges the quick-fire openings of Acts I and II for a sombre realisation of the sun gradually rising over a Californian forest. It is a passage more remarkable for the atmosphere it creates than for the memorability of its ideas. To that extent it is the complete reverse of *Tosca*, which attempts to invest almost every bead of perspiration with musical import. Puccini appears finally to have grasped the significance of the maxim that sometimes less is more.

As the excitement mounts in anticipation of Johnson's capture, Puccini takes a short-breathed motif – as was his increasing tendency towards the end of his career – and runs with it over and over to create the necessary intensity. Even Johnson's famous aria 'Ch'ella mi creda libero' ('Let her believe that I have gained my freedom'), in which he attempts to persuade the gang to let him go free, is more dignified than hysterically impassioned. Simply because Puccini never allows the emotional temperature to reach fever pitch, the final scene (the first of Puccini's operas not to end in tragedy) is all the more touching for its powerful restraint.

Yet if *La fanciulla* was Puccini's coming-of-age opera, his next venture was to achieve a level of suave sophistication and elegance that his detractors would scarcely have believed possible.

Chapter 9

Writing for the Enemy: *La rondine*

Writing for the Enemy: *La rondine*

Given both the time it had taken him to arrive at *La fanciulla del West* as a subject, and the effort of fashioning it into an opera, Puccini would have surprised no one had he elected to take some time off. Furthermore, his marriage had been put under severe strain by the Doria affair, and the challenge of producing a work quite different from anything he had so far produced had cost Puccini dear. He lacked the easy facility and creative drive of composers like Saint-Saëns, who claimed to produce music 'as an apple tree produces apples'. Yet before Puccini had completed work on *La fanciulla* he was already searching for ideas that might fire his imagination for his next project.

Ever since his first opera *Le villi* had opened in Milan, Puccini had keenly nurtured his own work. His devotion to each of his musical 'children' was virtually unprecedented as he travelled constantly to make sure that important new productions came up to the mark. Now that the composer was getting a little older, Tito Ricordi was called in to assist, and it was into his hands that Puccini entrusted follow-up productions of *La fanciulla* in Boston and Chicago.

On Boxing Day 1910, just two weeks after the opera's world premiere, Puccini set sail on board the *Lusitania* bound for England. Here he spent two days in London where his social engagements included dinner with his compatriot, the inventor Guglielmo Marconi, who had recently received the Nobel prize for physics. He returned to London in May to supervise rehearsals for the Covent Garden premiere of *La fanciulla* and the following month was in Rome for a production conducted by Toscanini. Critics continued to wonder about Puccini's stylistic change of direction, yet audiences in the main were very appreciative. In August he visited Brescia, in early October Liverpool (to see an English-language performance of his reduced score for small orchestra), and then back to Italy and Naples.

Puccini still managed to indulge his passion for hunting in Torre del Lago, and as his bank balance swelled to great proportions, his tastes in outdoor pursuits became more indulgent. During the summer months he managed to have a week away with Elvira, touring the Tyrol by car; but his real thrill lay in sailing the high seas in his motor boat *Ricochet*, and most especially his latest prized possession, a top-of-the-range yacht which he named *Cio-Cio-San*. Puccini found the speeds of the latest cars and boats intoxicating, but remained more of an amateur enthusiast than an expert. Just as he had managed to get his first car into a ditch, on one occasion he succeeded in ramming a rowing-boat full of his family, sending them flying into the water. Thanks to the immediate attention of local fishermen no one was seriously hurt. Other favourite gadgets included an early radio set, which Puccini adored playing around with, a motorbike with sidecar, and one of the first telephones in Torre del Lago.

1911 passed by fairly uneventfully, but 1912 was not without its hiatuses. In April Puccini's sister Ramelde died following a short illness, and two months later Giulio Ricordi also passed away. Whatever issues had divided publisher and composer over the years, particularly as regards *Madama Butterfly*, Giulio had been Puccini's most loyal and vociferous supporter. Puccini had dallied over projects in a manner that would have severely tried anyone's patience, yet Ricordi had stood by his musical son. The new director of the firm was Giulio's son Tito, and although business continued smoothly enough things were never quite the same again.

A pall of gloom was cast that year by the publication of a pamphlet written by the critic Fausto Torrefranca entitled *Puccini e l'opera internazionale*. More propagandist than rigorous, its central tenet was that following Monteverdi Italian music had taken a 300-year wrong turn down a cul-de-sac marked 'opera'. Now a new group of composers born between 1875 and 1885 (the *generazione dell'ottanta*) was emerging – Respighi, Castelnuovo-Tedesco, Casella, Pizzetti and Malipiero. Their aim was to put Italian instrumental music back on the map. Even Verdi did not emerge unscathed. Puccini, however, was singled out for particular criticism as a bourgeois cosmopolitan whose art represented the dying embers of a burnt-out genre.

Although fanatically one-sided, Torrefranca was more in touch with the current scene than traditionalists were prepared to concede. Opera had indeed come to dominate Italian musical taste to the detriment of the symphony, string quartet and sonata, and Puccini undeniably represented the end of the great line of Italian operatic composers. Changes were also underway. From today's vantage point we can see the history of twentieth-century Italian music characterised by its gradual merging into the European mainstream, whether it be via the symphonic poems of Ottorino Respighi, the exuberantly tuneful concertos of Castelnuovo-Tedesco, or the other-worldly musical landscapes of Luciano Berio and Luigi Nono.

Of more pressing importance for Puccini was his ever-complicated personal life. By the end of 1911 he had entered into yet another extra-marital affair, this time with Baroness Josephine von Stängel, whom he appears to have first encountered during a trip to Paris. Puccini was fifty-four years old and hardly in the prime of life, whereas Josephine was thirty-five, and married with two daughters. What started out as a mild flirtation (Puccini must have been flattered to find himself the subject of attention from such a young and charming woman) soon escalated into full-blown passion.

Whatever obfuscations Puccini had employed to prevent his wife discovering his previous indiscretions, they were nothing compared to now. There was a 'boating holiday' to Viareggio, a 'research' trip to Munich, and a visit to the spa at Carlsbad to 'ease his diabetes'. He even went so far as to invite Josephine to accompany him to the Bayreuth Festival where he narrowly avoided being discovered by Cosima Wagner. Clearly the danger of carrying on an illicit relationship was all part of its thrill.

Almost certainly inspired by Josephine, Puccini composed his first music in two years, the song *Sogno d'or*, an enchanting lullaby of blissful serenity. Evidence as to just how seriously Josephine was taking the relationship is provided by her starting divorce proceedings against her husband the following April. Despite Elvira's growing suspicions, the liaison continued beyond the outbreak of the Great War, even though Josephine became a political enemy of state when Italy joined the Allies in May 1915; Lake Lugano was the couple's politically neutral meeting place. Puccini generously supported Josephine after her husband was killed in action on the Western Front, but in the end, following several hair-raising near escapes from the ever-watchful eye of Elvira and the Italian authorities, the affair simply fizzled out. It seems that Josephine found herself a handsome Italian army officer, which effectively put an end to it.

Meanwhile, January 1913 witnessed the La Scala premiere of *La fanciulla* which appears to have inspired in Puccini almost Tchaikovskyan levels of neurosis. During the preparations he hit one of his dark patches and became so despairing about what he considered the total incompetence of everyone involved that he wished his life was over. In the event everything went well and he ended up praising the production to the skies as though he had never been remotely concerned.

Though privately wounded and pitched into a bout of critical self-examination by the Torrefranca attack, Puccini offered no public riposte. In a way, he didn't need to: he was still riding on a wave of popular success. Puccini was in Hamburg during October to see *La fanciulla* safely performed there for the first time, although it was a visit to Vienna that was to provide the year's most unexpected event. Puccini was wined and dined by the city's most celebrated musicians, who included the Korngolds (critic Julius and his son Erich, who later found fame as one of Hollywood's finest screen composers) and operetta supremo, Franz Lehár. Then he was introduced to the director of the Carltheater, Siegmund Eibenshütz, who made him an offer he simply couldn't refuse. For the princely sum of 200,000 kronen Eibenshütz commissioned Puccini to write an operetta based on a text by Alfred Maria Willner. By April the following year the subject had been agreed: *Die Schwalbe* ('The Swallow'), which would henceforth become known under its Italian name *La rondine*.

Puccini had composed hardly anything over the previous three and a half years; but, with opera his chosen field, the search for the right libretto was absolutely crucial and there was nothing to be gained by exhausting false starts. The remarkable thing is that despite the prolonged rests between works, Puccini seemed able to compose at will whenever the situation required – in spite of his claims to the contrary.

Accordingly, it would be wrong to assume that between the premiere of *La fanciulla* in December 1910 and the go-ahead for *La rondine* in the spring of 1914 Puccini had been idle in deciding upon his next operatic subject. Indeed, there had been a constant flow of ideas and rejections throughout this period – including Maurice Maeterlinck's *L'Oiseau bleu* (the source for Debussy's opera, *Pelléas et Mélisande*), *Two Little Wooden Shoes* by Marie Louise de la Ramée (who wrote under the pseudonym Ouida), and *Anima allegra* by Joaquín and Serafín Álvarez Quintero. The latter, with its gypsy locations and its focus on an enchanting young girl, had all the makings of the light-hearted fare that Puccini had begun to think should form the basis of his next opus. He was put in contact with the young playwright Giuseppe Adami, and the two immediately got on. Adami, a skilled writer, was both flexible and amenable, and found no difficulty in translating Puccini's ideas into prose. He got as far as producing a draft libretto, but by the spring of 1912 Puccini was getting cold feet. For him, Bizet's *Carmen* had defined everything that a female-driven gypsy opera should be and he decided not to invite comparisons.

Until *La rondine* entered the ring in the spring of 1914, the only project that had truly gripped Puccini's imagination was Didier Gold's gruesome tale *La Houppelande* ('The Cloak'), a production of which Puccini saw in 1912 at the Théâtre Marigny in Paris. He had immediately snapped up the rights to the work, but put it on the back burner until the time was right.

During this particularly exasperating period of operatic trials and rejections, Puccini struck up a friendship with the Hungarian writer Margit Vészi. Like Sybil Seligman, Vészi was an emotional safety valve and confidante who again 'understood' the composer more than Elvira ever could. In a letter of April 1913 Puccini poured out his soul unguardedly:

> *My mind is black today!! I would like to be able to fly to your studio and speak to you, for I feel my spirit would find an echo in yours. You are the only person who knows how to weigh me down to the last milligram. You have an intuition about me and about all the strange nuances of my temperament... And for my art, which comes so much from the soul, I really need a guide, a spirit who will understand me, and you could be this counsellor.*

Relations had meanwhile become strained between Puccini and Tito Ricordi, whose enthusiasm for Riccardo Zandonai, the composer he considered to be the next golden boy of Italian opera, was denying Puccini the respect to which he felt entitled. At one stage Tito had even attempted to rush Puccini into signing a contract for a new project in which the composer had not the slightest interest. As a result Puccini agreed financial terms regarding *La rondine* with an Austrian publisher, and then in May 1914 commissioned Adami to write the scenario of Willner's original tale. By September the work was already taking shape and Puccini informed Sybil Seligman that 'It's a light sentimental opera with touches of comedy – but it's agreeable, limpid, easy to sing with a little waltz music and lively and fetching tunes.'

There were the inevitable wranglings and heated discussions along the way regarding the libretto (in November 1914 Puccini dismissed the whole thing as 'trash' and a year later described himself as 'vomiting over the score'), so it wasn't until nearly two years later, in April 1916, that *La rondine* was finally completed. There had, of course, been similar delays during Puccini's previous operatic ventures due largely to creative differences, the composer's notoriously relaxed approach to his work, and assorted domestic problems. This time, schedules went to pieces because in the summer of 1914 war broke out in Europe.

In the light of the countless lives lost in the trenches during the conflict, it is easy to view as crass Puccini's initial worries about whether *La rondine* would ever be performed or whether he should abandon the project altogether. Yet no one in Italy,

Puccini with Tito Ricordi

least of all the apolitical Puccini, had the slightest notion of the scale of human tragedy that would eventually unfold. 'War is a terrible thing,' Puccini wrote to Sybil, 'whatever the results, for whether it be victory or defeat, human lives are sacrificed.'

For now it was bad enough that Austro-German ill feeling was already running high. Thanks to Puccini's contract with the Viennese, he was forced to walk a tightrope between supporting the Allies and not causing offence to the Germans. At one point Paris looked set to remove Puccini's music from the schedules altogether until his eleventh-hour intervention of waiving all royalties for performances of *Tosca* at the Opéra Comique in support of the Allied war effort. A blazing row then erupted between Puccini and the fiercely nationalistic Toscanini, the upshot of which being that the two men barely spoke to one another for several years. Toscanini saw war in terms of opposing countries, winners and losers. For Puccini it was the totality of human carnage that was so depressing.

Desperate to find a way of extricating himself from the contract with Vienna, Puccini tried to convince Eibenshütz (not without some justification) that Adami's libretto had altered the perspectives and detail of the original to such an extent that it was now barely recognisable. This had no effect, however, and the rights to the first performance in German remained with the Austrians.

Puccini now played his ace. Tito Ricordi had backed away from associating himself with *La rondine*, partly due to reservations about the work and partly because he would have had to negotiate with 'enemy' nationals. Accordingly, Lorenzo Sonzogno leapt at the chance of acquiring both the publication rights and the rights to the first performance outside Austria; this effectively meant that the world premiere could now take place as long as it was given in Italian. Monte Carlo was chosen as the ideal venue (Monaco being a neutral state), and Puccini scored a political coup by claiming that he had effectively wrestled *La rondine* back from the Austrians. To underline his devotion to the Allied cause he freely contributed the song *Morire?* to a volume that Ricordi was publishing in aid of the Italian Red Cross.

Finally, with all political and contractual obstructions successfully removed, the world premiere of *La rondine* was given on 27 March 1917 in the Monte Carlo Opera House with Gilda dalla Rizza (whom Puccini admired enormously) as Magda and the great Tito Schipa as Ruggero, under the baton of Gino Marinuzzi. Despite the work's experimental nature (with Puccini reining in any hint of *verismo* melodrama and achieving a feather-light deftness in his waltz rhythms to rival those of Strauss's *Der Rosenkavalier* and Lehár's *Merry*

Widow) it was an instant success – and one of the most fulfilling triumphs of Puccini's career.

It was only when *La rondine* moved to Italy that the problems began. The public in general adored its insatiable bonhomie, but the critics denounced its easy flow of waltz tunes and its frivolous plot, deriding Puccini for apparently having written it merely for the generous commission. For example, Puccini had been concerned about the standard of musical preparation for the Milan premiere; the critics disagreed but went out of their way to lambaste the score, *Il Secolo* reporting: 'That poor excuse for music is neither vivacious nor of a sufficiently popular character to be described as an operetta, nor is it elevated enough to be called a lyric comedy'. The composer set to work on a revised version, which, three years later, in April 1920, went down moderately well in Palermo. Vienna would finally get to see *Die Schwalbe* on 7 October 1920, but once again its reception was respectable rather than enthusiastic. As a result Puccini made further revisions, although this third and final version would have to wait until 1994 before being premiered – in Turin. The Metropolitan Opera didn't stage *La rondine* until 1928, four years after Puccini's death, and the Royal Opera House, Covent Garden only raised the curtain on this irresistible gem as recently as 2002. Even now, only two of Puccini's operas are performed less often than *La rondine*: *Le villi* and *Edgar*.

Gilda dalla Rizza

The key to appreciating *La rondine*'s very special qualities lies in listening to it as an exquisite distillation of Puccini's creative personality. It is here that his conversational style of composing reaches its apogee and his orchestration is at its most subtle and supple. Not since *La Bohème* had Puccini achieved such a sense of irrepressible spontaneity, of the music pouring onwards in one unstoppable flow. Using the waltz as a background he continually delights the senses with the distinctive harmonic turns and melodic succulence of yore, but suffused with a pleasing restraint. *La rondine* is also by far and away Puccini's most romantically idealised work.

If ever Puccini can be said to have achieved perfection it is in the first act – a glorious summation of the composer's art sustained at such a high level that one wishes it would go on for ever. The delights come so thick and fast, it seems as though they might fall over one another in an effort to be heard. 'Chi' il bel sogno di Doretta' ('Who could guess the beautiful dream of Doretta?'), with its chains of gentle suspensions and added-note chords, is one of the most perfectly balanced and easily assimilated melodies that even Puccini composed. For his scene-setting music at its most inspired one need look no further than the episode introducing Ruggero, which entwines waltzing luxuriance with a playful delight in timbre and texture and is thus briefly reminiscent of Ravel's children's opera, *L'Enfant et les sortilèges*.

Here is a further clue to unlocking the secrets of *La rondine*. As in the opera by Ravel, and Stravinsky's ballet *Petrushka* (the score of which Puccini saw before starting work on the opera), there is an element of the marionette about *La rondine*'s characters. One wouldn't go so far as to describe them as mere ciphers, although Puccini succeeds in making them as stylised as the story itself. Reversing the principles of *La Bohème*, in which a simple story is writ

La rondine

Act I: The France of Napoleon III, in the 1850s; a dinner party is in full swing at the Parisian salon of Magda, a courtesan. The poet Prunier is regaling a group of admiring ladies with his opinions on the latest fad for 'romantic love'. It is just a passing phase, he insists, although Magda takes it more seriously. Prunier points out that even the heroine of his latest verses, Doretta, dreams of a king who offers her riches in return for affection. That, apparently, is as far as Prunier has got. Magda suggests an ending in which Doretta finds true love.

Magda's lover, Rambaldo, joins in the discussion, insisting that falling in love is a weakness, one that he has successfully guarded against. As if to prove his point he presents Magda with a luxurious necklace which she accepts, while still insisting that true love is possible and that money can't buy everything. Ruggero, the son of one of Rambaldo's childhood friends, is announced just as Prunier begins to read Magda's palm. He explains that like a swallow she will always fly towards love, but that what will happen next is far from clear. Ruggero meanwhile asks about Paris's main attractions. It is decided that he should first visit Bullier's nightclub, and members of the group go their separate ways. However, once Ruggero has left, Magda dashes upstairs, changes into clothes more suited to a working-class girl and heads for Bullier's where she clearly hopes to find 'love'. Meanwhile we see Prunier meet Magda's maid, Lisette, with whom he is having a secret affair. The couple also head in the direction of the famous night club.

Act II: In the ballroom at Bullier's, where Magda arrives and makes contact with Ruggero, who fails to recognise her in her ordinary clothes (she tells him her name is 'Paulette'). The two discover a mutual attraction and as they embrace they are spotted by Prunier and Lisette. The latter is convinced the woman is Magda but Prunier tactfully insists that she is mistaken. Champagne is ordered and upon its arrival the two couples drink a toast in celebration of love. Just as the emotional temperature rises Rambaldo walks in. Despite the others' stern warnings Magda confronts Rambaldo and announces that their affair is over – she is now in love with Ruggero. Rambaldo departs, and Magda ponders on what the future may bring as she leaves with her new lover.

Act III: A villa on the Riviera where Magda and Ruggero discuss their plans for the future. Ruggero has written to his father for money and asked for his blessing to marry Magda, who is rather taken aback given her previous life as a courtesan. Lisette and Prunier arrive on the scene somewhat deflated as a result of Lisette's failure to become a successful singer. Prunier asks Magda to take Lisette back in her old role as maid while pointing out that all her old friends are missing her and hoping she might return. Meanwhile Ruggero has received a letter from his mother in which she gives her blessing to the marriage so long as Magda is faithful and pure. On reading this Magda realises that the whole affair has been an illusion and that her place is indeed back with her friends in Paris. Despite Ruggero's protestations she turns and departs, leaving him distraught with grief.

large, Puccini doesn't attempt in *La rondine* to make the drama carry any more emotional weight than is absolutely necessary. Viewed in this way, the final act, which is often dismissed as the weakest of the three, is not about increasing tension or resolving the huge dilemmas of an imposing story arc but should be experienced almost as one might experience a play in a puppet theatre.

In many respects *La rondine* stands outside the mainstream opera and operetta traditions. It will never be one of Puccini's more popular works, and even the composer appears to have despaired of it in later life. Aesthetically speaking it is the most sophisticated of his operas: it underlined his ability to keep reinventing himself as well as providing further evidence of his readiness to absorb ideas from fellow composers. Yet for all the work's sublime qualities, and despite the six years it took to bring it to fruition, it was never the money-spinner its immediate predecessors had been. Puccini needed something new – and he needed it fast.

Chapter 10

Three for the Price of One:
Il trittico

Three for the Price of One: *Il trittico*

Aware that *La rondine* was not blockbuster material, Puccini had been quietly working away on another project at the same time. Initially planned as a pairing of two contrasted works (one light-hearted, the other tragic), it was in fact an idea that Puccini had suggested to Giulio Ricordi several years before: a grand operatic trilogy to be performed in a single evening.

The first work to fall into place was an adaptation of Gold's *La Houppelande*, to which Puccini had already secured the rights. He wrote excitedly to the trusty Illica that 'The subject is *apache* in every way... rather Grand Guignol, but that doesn't matter. It pleases me and strikes me as highly effective.' Following unsuccessful try-outs with both Giovacchino Forzano and Ferdinando Martini, in the late autumn of 1913 Puccini turned finally to Adami, who had adapted the Quintero brothers' *Anima allegra* for him the previous year. Adami had the whole thing ready in only one week, his speed the deciding factor in Puccini's request that he prepare the libretto of *La rondine* the following spring. In 1914 Puccini's time was taken up exclusively with *La rondine*, but once the larger work was completed Puccini turned immediately to *Il tabarro* (as Gold's work was now known, 'il tabarro' meaning 'The Cloak'); he finished it in November 1916, four months before *La rondine*'s premiere.

The opening of *Il tabarro*, with its parallel 4ths and veiled textures, is hauntingly reminiscent of Debussy, while the lapping of the river and its rippling surface is unmistakably suggested by the constant compound swaying of quavers – perhaps the music here is a distillation of Puccini's years spent listening to the sounds of water lapping the shores of his home at Torre del Lago. If *La rondine* took the dancing of *La Bohème* to new levels of emotional restraint and poetic refinement, so *Il tabarro* returns us, in part, to the dark, *verismo* world of *Tosca*, but now with greater subtlety. As in *Tosca* we sense the impending doom almost continuously, even when the music turns playful with the sound of the hurdy-gurdy, which is convincingly realised through the use of deliberately 'mistuned' intervals for two flutes, two clarinets and bass clarinet. Puccini even plays an in-joke on himself by introducing strands from *La Bohème* where the ballad-monger sings the story of Mimì.

Other felicitous touches include the delicious imitation of a cat from the oboes and violas as La Frugola sings 'Se tu sapessi' ('If you only knew'); and the music's insistent, monotonal quality as she dreams of owning a cottage in the country possesses a stabbing insistence (one can almost imagine her issuing orders to her husband) rather than the expected nostalgic longing. Most notably, Puccini's flowing style reaches new levels of integration so that even when solos do emerge from the near-continuous textures (like the river itself, the music seems truly unending) they do so completely naturally.

The first half of *Il tabarro* is an exhilarating series of virtuoso sleights of hand, but when the fun and games are over and Luigi initially approaches Giorgetta for a cuddle, there is a distinct change in atmosphere. Puccini has so far indulged his inspiration in broad sweeps, whereas now uncertainty prevails, with lyrical phrases not allowed to flower openly and thereby suggesting the secrecy of the love tryst.

Il tabarro

The River Seine, Paris, 1910. A barge skippered by the middle-aged Michele is moored safely. As the deckhands – Luigi, Tinca and Talpa – offload the vessel's cargo, Michele asks for a kiss from his young wife, Giorgetta. She responds but without affection, offering wine to their helpers. While Michele is briefly away, an organ grinder begins to play and Giorgetta dances first with Luigi then Tinca, before Michele's return brings their light-heartedness to an abrupt end. Giorgetta asks her husband why he seems so distracted but he refuses to answer.

Talpa's wife, La Frugola, arrives to collect him and they dream of one day owning their own cottage in the country. Talpa wants nothing more than to drown his sorrows in drink, Luigi bemoans his existence as a stevedore, and Giorgetta wishes she could leave the barge and return to the Parisian suburb where she was raised as a child. As they go their separate ways, Giorgetta and Luigi are briefly left alone together and it is revealed that they are lovers. Their ardour is interrupted by Michele's re-emergence from the cabin. Luigi, who cannot stand sharing Giorgetta with another man, asks to be dropped off at Rouen the next day, but Michele persuades him to stay on. Once Michele has retired for the night, Giorgetta and Luigi arrange to meet later – her signal will be a lighted match.

Michele reappears on deck and, sensing his wife's disquiet, attempts to rekindle their former love for one another, reminding her of better days before their child died when he used to wrap them both up warmly in his cloak. His attempts are rebuffed, however, leaving him to ponder, as he lights his pipe, whether she might be having an affair and with whom. Luigi sees the light and responds as arranged. Michele grabs him by the throat, forcing a confession out of him before strangling him and wrapping his body in his cloak. Giorgetta comes out on deck to apologise to Michele, whereupon he triumphantly opens the cloak and reveals Luigi's dead body.

The nervous juxtaposition of contrasting moods and types of musical articulation adds significantly to the growing sense of menace. As in the opening prelude this is not writing that forms a mere backdrop to what is happening, but writing that becomes a vital part of the action through its various shapes and colours. It is also fascinating to compare the cosmopolitan writing of the first half (with its hints of Debussy, Ravel, Stravinsky and Richard Strauss), with the second, which, as the tension increases, reverts to a more distinctly Italianate form of melodrama.

Yet even here there is a difference. *Tosca* is almost literal in its depiction of violent depravity, but in *Il tabarro* there is a haunting malevolence – what Puccini referred to as 'grand guignol' – that finds a strange parallel in Schoenberg's Expressionist period. More than any other of Puccini's works, *Il tabarro* possesses a claustrophobic quality that sucks in the audience so that they are not so much observing events as actually caught up in them (this is the complete opposite of Verdi's tendency to take an opera out to its audience). When Giorgetta cries out upon seeing her lover's lifeless corpse rolled out like an animal carcass, we experience her feelings as acutely as if they were our own.

Puccini despaired of ever finding suitable companions for *Il tabarro*, and even considered at one point putting it on as a double feature with *Le villi*. However, in January 1917, still two months before the premiere of *La rondine*, Forzano stepped into the breach with an idea of his own: a religious tale entitled *Suor Angelica* ('Sister Angelica'), which he originally envisaged as a straightforward dramatic production. Puccini took to the story immediately and with very little fuss set to work. In what, by his standards, was a veritable explosion of creativity, he had *Suor Angelica* fully composed and orchestrated in nine months.

This was doubly remarkable as not only had Puccini to deal with all the preparations and aftermath associated with *La rondine*, he had decided to run with another suggestion of Forzano's – about the Florentine scoundrel *Gianni Schicchi* as described in Dante's *Inferno*. This was, at last, just the comedy Puccini had been looking for. After some initial doubts he fell under the story's spell to such an extent that for a while during the summer of 1917 he ceased work on *Suor Angelica* to get the new project underway. Again with the maximum of concentrated effort, *Gianni Schicchi* was completed on 20 April 1918. The three operas are almost entirely unconnected both dramatically and musically, yet it was planned that they be performed together, and the title eventually settled upon was *Il trittico* ('The Triptych').

Suor Angelica has been heavily criticised for its saccharine storyline, apparent lack of dramatic intensity, and for the overheated religiosity of its final scene. For listeners of a certain age, associations with the idealised convent scenes and singing nuns in *The Sound of Music* are at times hard to avoid, although in many ways this is the key that unlocks the door to this much-maligned work. Puccini was writing when the cinema was still in its infancy, 'talkies' were a decade away, and the golden age of Hollywood scores from the likes of Korngold, Steiner, Rózsa and Waxman was another ten years after that. Puccini's achievement was to capture the idealism of the nuns in music – of radiant contentment – that seems to be tracing their thoughts.

Like a modern film score the music complements and drives forward the action with an at times onomatopoeic alliance. There are shades of Strauss's *Don Quixote* and *An Alpine Symphony* when during Sister Genovieffa's 'Soave Signor mio' ('My sweet Lord') the woodwind section suggests a herd of bleating sheep, and Sister Clara's wasp sting is evoked

Suor Angelica

A convent near Siena towards the end of the seventeenth century. Sister Angelica and two lay sisters are late for chapel and are chided by the Monitor. As the sisterhood gathers in the courtyard there is general rejoicing: this is one of only three evenings a year when the rays of the setting sun strike the fountain, turning the water to liquid gold.

Moved by the sensual pleasure of the fountain's transformation, the nuns' thoughts turn to more worldly things, much to the Monitor's disapproval. Sister Genovieffa wishes that she could see the spring lambs again, and Sister Dolcina that she could indulge her epicurean desires. Sister Angelica claims not to be affected by such thoughts, although this merely sets the other nuns gossiping about the noble family from whom Angelica has heard nothing in seven years and who, it seems, banished her to the convent by way of a punishment.

Word is received that a luxurious coach has pulled up at the convent gate bearing a distinguished-looking visitor. Angelica becomes noticeably agitated at the news, only to be chastised by the Abbess for her unseemly behaviour. The mysterious stranger turns out to be Angelica's aunt, the Princess, who coolly explains that Angelica's sister, Anna, is about to be married. As trustee of the family's fortune (following the death of Angelica's parents), she commands that Angelica signs her share over to Anna.

It seems that Angelica had given birth to an illegitimate son seven years earlier and as a result of the shame she brought on her family was sent to the convent. Angelica feels she has already repented enough for her mistake, but when she is told her son died two years earlier from fever she breaks down and signs the document, thereby relinquishing her inheritance. She resolves to join her son in heaven, but, having taken a draught of poison, realises that she has committed a cardinal sin and begs the Virgin Mary for forgiveness. As she collapses, dying, she sees a vision of the Blessed Virgin with Angelica's son at her side welcoming her through the gates of heaven.

by pizzicato strings and muted trumpets. More importantly, with the exception of one or two mild outbursts, the emotional contours are kept within a tight range almost unprecedented in any of Puccini's other works. His aim was to compose music that fully reflected the calm existence of the nuns' daily lives. Only the music for the two characters who don't really belong in the convent – Suor Angelica and her aunt the Princess – produces writing of heightened melodrama; a striking contrast is thereby created between those of worldly outlook and those whose existence is governed by the spiritual. The Princess's first entrance is a particularly chilling portrayal that serrates the atmosphere with the jagged edge of worldly wisdom. And Angelica evokes the death of her young son in the unforgettable and passionate solo, 'Senza mamma' – an extended aria not fixed in its form until after the vocal score was engraved.

The final scene has been criticised for its failure to capture the transfiguration with sufficient ethereal spiritual uplift. To say, as has been claimed, that Puccini was simply incapable of such a thing is to miss the point. Puccini was an Italian first and foremost, yet musically his special brand of emotionalism owed much to the Russian school (Mussorgsky via Tchaikovsky) and it is this which is recalled in the fever-pitch ending. In Puccini's opinion, *Suor Angelica* was the finest of the three operas and it is at such a moment that he reveals the real man within. He could easily have climbed serenely into the heavens, yet he chose to root the music in symbolic simplicity, in terms of the peasant and the altar.

By comparison, *Gianni Schicchi* is a light-hearted comedy, and, compared to the time-suspending, dream-like quality of *Suor Angelica*, it is a high-speed drama. Underlying the deft ingenuity with which Puccini moves us from one rapid encounter to another – one minute skipping along in jocular fashion, lyrically opulent the next – is the fall of the interval of a major 2nd. At times it possesses a throwaway, carefree quality, at others it is more reflective, and at others it is the equivalent of a musical sigh.

The frenetic action has drawn comparisons with Verdi's *Falstaff*; the two operas share a bucolic quality and Verdi's final masterpiece was certainly an important influence. Yet whereas the older composer's work owes much to the blustering style of *opera buffa*, Puccini uses a wider stylistic and musical range: nothing in *Falstaff* remotely compares with Lauretta's 'O mio babbino caro' ('Oh, my beloved father'), a slow and sentimental lyric into which Puccini pours all his melodic gifts. Less famous, but rather impressive and also unlike anything in *Falstaff*, is Rinuccio's 'Firenze è come un albero fiorito' ('Florence is like a flowering tree'). Additionally, Verdi plays for laughs much of the time, whereas Puccini sets the comic elements in a real-life context. Puccini's opera is largely about ordinary characters (save for the title role) playing out a comically ridiculous situation; Verdi's is fundamentally about larger-than-life, loveable rogues behaving comically. Puccini's humour has a sting in its tail.

Although Puccini would have loved dearly to premiere *Il trittico* in Rome, this was clearly impossible with war still raging in Europe. In the end he settled on an invitation from New York to stage the premiere at the Metropolitan Opera on 14 December 1918, although he was unable to attend; despite the Armistice having just been concluded, the Atlantic was still awash with unexploded mines. Some fine singers were assembled, including Giulio Crimi, who played both Rinuccio in *Gianni Schicchi* and Luigi in *Il tabarro*, Claudia Muzio as Giorgetta, Giuseppe de Luca as Gianni Schicchi and Geraldine Farrar as Suor Angelica. The

Gianni Schicchi

The gold-digging relatives of Buoso Donati have gathered around his death-bed in his Florentine palace. The rumour is that he left his considerable fortune to a monastery, but since his last will and testament has not been filed with a notary there begins a frenzied search to uncover the document. Rinuccio, Zita's twenty-four-year-old nephew, finds it and asks his aunt, whether, if he's been left sufficient funds, he can marry his beloved Lauretta, Gianni Schicchi's daughter. But when the will is opened they discover to their horror that Donati did indeed leave his fortune to the monks.

Rinuccio suggests in his aria 'Firenze è come un albero fiorito' that only Schicchi, one of a new breed of peasants who has done well for himself, can find a way of saving the situation. The rest of the family, considering Schicchi to be a country bumpkin, refuses to have anything to do with him at first. Eventually they change their minds, but then it is Schicchi's turn to refuse to have anything to do with them due to their selfish greed. He is about to turn and leave when Lauretta announces her love for Rinuccio in the unforgettable aria 'O mio babbino caro'. Schicchi relents, agrees to take a look at the will, and hatches a plan whereby the family keeps Donati's death a secret and he (Schicchi) impersonates him and writes a new will himself.

Once the body has been removed, Schicchi dons nightcap and gown and listens to each potential inheritor in turn describe what he or she hopes to get out of the will, making each one swear to complete secrecy. When the notary arrives, Schicchi dictates that five florins should go to the monks, some farmland and associated buildings to the family, and that the bulk of the estate should go to Gianni Schicchi. The relatives, quite naturally, are apoplectic at Schicchi's deception but there is nothing they can do. Eventually they are herded out of the building, leaving Rinuccio and Lauretta to embrace and Schicchi to gaze with satisfaction upon how the money was eventually spent.

conductor, Roberto Moranzoni, was personally coached by Puccini for three months before curtain-up.

Il tabarro, despite being arguably the finest of the three on account of its structural coherence and skilful orchestration, didn't inspire much interest from the critics, while *Suor Angelica* was derided for its 'Christmas-card presentation' and lack of anything new. At least the comedy *Gianni Schicchi* enjoyed some success, largely as a result of the show-stopping 'O mio babbino caro'. In fact, the aria sounds rather out of place in context but it gave the audience just about the only glimpse of the standard, soaring Puccini aria that his fans had come to know and love, and which was conspicuously missing from *Il tabarro*.

The Italian premiere was given less than a month later on 11 January 1919 in Rome's Teatro Costanzi. Once again *Gianni Schicchi* emerged as the firm favourite, although the Italians took more kindly to the gentle goings-on of *Suor Angelica*, finding the *verismo* brutality of *Il tabarro* decidedly passé. Clearly the age of *Cavalleria rusticana* and *I pagliacci* was almost past. Despite Puccini's fervent desire that the three operas should be performed together, within two years of the 1919 premiere *Suor Angelica* and (to a lesser extent) *Il tabarro* had virtually fallen by the wayside. Toscanini, who was still smarting from the heated political debate with Puccini during the early days of the war, hardly helped matters when he announced publicly that as far as *Il tabarro* was concerned he 'didn't like it at all'. Interestingly, in an anonymous article published in the *Idea nazionale* in 1919, the writer (probably the same Fausto Torrefranca who in 1912 had savaged Puccini in his essay) delivers a backhanded compliment to Puccini for ramping up his use of contemporary compositional techniques in *Il trittico* 'as his inspiration began to lose its imaginative invention'.

Draft score of
Gianni Schicchi

Toscanini was originally invited by Covent Garden to conduct the British premiere in the summer of 1920, but Puccini forbade it, referring to his former friend and supporter as 'that *pig*' in his correspondence. In the event Puccini supervised rehearsals himself, and, when Thomas

Beecham turned down an invitation to conduct, the Italian Gaetano Bavagnoli was brought in for the gala premiere, at which King George V and Queen Mary were present. Puccini himself was rapturously received, but *Suor Angelica* once again proved the lame duck; after the second full performance *Il trittico* was unceremoniously dropped from the schedule altogether.

The following year, while supervising rehearsals in Bologna, Puccini moaned about the triptych's 'transatlantic cable' length, although he remained firmly wedded to the overall concept. As with much of his later work, the circumstances surrounding the operas were significant. *Il tabarro*'s striking advances in textural lucidity and harmonic ingenuity were largely ignored, not only because the general opera-going public considered *verismo* dead in the water, but also because Puccini's die-hard fans still hungered for more of his opulent, turn-of-the-century style. *Suor Angelica* was composed as an intermezzo, a relatively gentle piece that would link the brooding violence of *Il tabarro* with the frothy light-heartedness of *Gianni Schicchi*. The tendency of audiences and critics of the time, however, was to view it as an entirely separate entity divorced from its surroundings. *Gianni Schicchi* suited far better the mood of the times, its gentle comedy providing a vital tonic to the doom and gloom of war-torn Europe. It was also something that opera audiences already understood: one-act comic operas had been in existence since Rossini's sparkling early masterworks such as *La scala di seta* and *Il Signor Bruschino*.

The problem with *Il trittico* has nothing to do with paucity of ideas; on the contrary, it lies in the difficulty audiences have in absorbing Puccini's utterly different approaches to the three scenarios. *Il tabarro* is so dense and compressed in its emotional power that it seems capable of expanding beyond its temporal boundaries. *Suor Angelica* operates in a quite different way, feeling completely settled in its miniature surroundings. *Gianni Schicchi* exhibits an alternative kind of compression, one in which the speed of delivery and quick-fire chain of events are all part of the comic effect. All this gives audiences experiencing the trilogy for the first time rather a lot to deal with in just one hearing.

The gramophone age has brought about a profound reassessment of *Il trittico*. Not only has it given listeners the chance to become more familiar with these works individually, but it has also provided the opportunity to move through the trilogy with ease. Although it is still unusual to find performances of *Il trittico* given complete in one evening, a growing number of commentators now consider *Il tabarro* to be Puccini's finest contribution to the world of opera.

Chapter 11

A Glorious Sunset and a New Dawn: *Turandot*

A Glorious Sunset and a New Dawn: *Turandot*

When Italy had entered the Great War in 1915, Puccini had initially tried his best to carry on as though nothing was happening. It was a forlorn attempt. Before the conflict was over he had fallen out with Toscanini, formerly one of his closest musical allies, over the direction the conflict was taking; and his love affair with a political enemy (Josephine von Stängel) and the contract for *La rondine* with an enemy country (Austria) had brought him into disrepute. He had been deeply affected by the war and its consequences, and now felt alien in a world that had changed irrevocably.

Everywhere, money was scarce and, for a luxurious pursuit such as opera, post-war uncertainty meant the possibility of productions being cancelled, opera houses closing down, and stars fleeing central Europe for America and Russia. However, after the cessation of hostilities, it was once again possible to perform certain operas in countries from which they had been banned for political reasons. Had *La rondine* and *Il trittico* been premiered under happier circumstances with the usual spate of first performances around the world, these still neglected gems might have earned a regular place in the repertoire, but under the circumstances there was little chance of a fresh start.

With the poor reception accorded his recent operas Puccini felt despondent over his work, and now his daily life was affected. He had initially hoped that a backwater such as Torre del Lago might survive the war more or less intact, but the government had erected a peat factory which sounded its noisy sirens several times a day and belched out disgusting-smelling fumes around the lake. Political thinking had also changed substantially: the traditional lower classes were no longer prepared to sit back and unquestioningly accept the behaviour of their 'betters'. As a privileged artist Puccini found himself in the firing line from the very same local peasants he once considered his drinking friends. The rise of socialism was making itself felt and at one point Puccini came close to having his hunting rights rescinded altogether.

Puccini's days at Torre were clearly numbered, yet at least one good thing came out of the immediate post-war period: a young priest named Dante Del Fiorentino, who had previously been little more than a passing acquaintance, came to work in Torre. The two men became firm friends, so much so that when Puccini did move away from Torre – making a new home in Viareggio in December 1921 – Del Fiorentino stayed in touch and kept an invaluable record of his many encounters with the composer during his final years. After the composer's death Del Fiorentino dedicated himself to creating an archive of material, including, most importantly, Puccini's correspondence with many of his local friends.

With his spirits at an all-time low, in 1919 Puccini was commissioned by the city fathers of Rome to compose a chest-beating paean to the glories of Italy's capital city. This work, which the composer himself described as a 'piece of trash', was produced merely to keep the politicians happy. It is written in much the same vein as Elgar's *Pomp and Circumstance* marches. The double premiere at two different

Puccini reading by the fireplace in his study in Viareggio

events on 21 April was called off when the heavens opened. Eventually *Inno a Roma* was performed on 1 June at the Royal Gymnastics Competition amid great pomp and ceremony. Puccini couldn't be bothered to turn up, yet it apparently went down very well. He certainly hoped that it would become popular: Sonzogno published it in 1923, with a dedication to Princess Jolanda di Savoia; later it would be embraced by Mussolini's Fascists.

Otherwise the year was taken up with visits to London, Paris and Vienna. Puccini was now sixty years of age, yet, despite everything, continued to look young for his age. Inevitably his thoughts turned to a suitable text on which to base his next operatic venture. There was initially an idea from Forzano for an opera based on the character Christopher Sly from Shakespeare's *The Taming of the Shrew*. Puccini decided against it (although it eventually appeared in operatic form as Wolf-Ferrari's *Sly,* premiered at La Scala in 1927).

Adami was then brought on board to help find a solution to the problem, along with the renowned critic Renato Simoni. Their initial suggestion was an adaptation of Dickens's *Oliver Twist* and they got as far as working on a treatment before this too was abandoned. Just as Puccini despaired of finding anything in the foreseeable future, Adami and Simoni invited him to lunch in Milan during March 1920 to present a new idea. Simoni was a scholar of the work of Carlo Gozzi and so it was perhaps inevitable that he would have suggested *Turandot*. Puccini was immediately hooked.

This wasn't the first time the story had been set. Puccini's old teacher Bazzini had composed *Turanda* in 1867 and as recently as 1917 Busoni made an operatic expansion of some incidental music he had composed for *Turandot* in 1911. As Busoni's objective aesthetic was the very antithesis of Puccini's rich humanity, there was never any possibility of their works sounding remotely similar. Accordingly, Adami and Simoni set to work on fashioning a libretto that Puccini specifically requested should 'make the world weep'.

Later in 1920 Puccini was in London to see the British premiere of *Il trittico* and then Vienna for the long-awaited premiere of *Die Schwalbe* (the German title of *La rondine*). Meanwhile the librettists continued toiling away on *Turandot*; although the first act seems to have gone fairly smoothly, the second and third acts proved tough-going, with Puccini being as exacting as ever. By the end of the year he had hit one of his habitual low winter spells and was wondering whether the opera would ever see the light of day.

Nevertheless, work continued apace and by April 1921 Puccini felt confident enough about the first act to start composing, if rather fitfully. By August most of the first act was complete and the second had been knocked into shape to his satisfaction. Then, just as everything seemed to be going well, Puccini had one of his characteristic changes of heart, and wanted the whole work restructured into two acts. Following countless heated discussions, by the end of the year *Turandot* had indeed been completely refashioned; it was still in three acts, but now with the original first act divided into two, and the second and third telescoped together. When one considers the finely balanced result his decision seems entirely obvious, but at the time it put the cat among the pigeons to an extent unrivalled since the heady days of working with Illica and Giacosa on *Madama Butterfly*.

Work on the new three-act *Turandot* was steady during the first half of 1922, despite Puccini's murmurs about a possible change of project altogether. Writing to Adami he complained:

> *I have no good news about* Turandot. *I am beginning to be worried about my laziness... I am certainly failing to write anything else that is good. Also I am old! Of that there is no doubt... Perhaps I shall return the money to Ricordi and cancel the contract... I have tried again and again to write the*

music for the introductory scene of Act II, and cannot. I don't
feel comfortable in China.

Nevertheless the orchestration of the first act was completed by November 1922, by which time the complete libretto had finally arrived – much to everyone's relief. Despite a dispute with Ricordi over the firm's allowing its American wing to publish a foxtrot version of the humming chorus from *Madama Butterfly* without the composer's permission, terms were eventually agreed and Puccini decided to sign *Turandot* over to the old firm. Two years in the making, the new libretto – with its themes of love, terror, sacrifice and riddles all set in ancient China – was as evocative a story as any Puccini had ever worked on.

With the first act nearing completion and the full libretto safely in his hands, Puccini set off on a leisurely motoring holiday through Austria, Germany, Holland and Switzerland. It was during this otherwise pleasant sojourn that he got a bone caught in his throat; it had to be surgically removed. Given his family's disposition to cancer, the previous incidence of throat problems, and now a wound that required surgery, there is a distinct possibility that it may have given rise to the tumour that would eventually kill him.

Puccini's return to Viareggio and his work lowered his mood considerably. His despondency about the general state of post-war Italy was hardly improved by the rise of Fascism under Mussolini. He was relieved that someone at least was recognising the problems and seemed willing to act. During a short meeting arranged with the dictator, however, he received absolutely no support for his operatic schemes – there was no money, he was told. Puccini's sympathies were, on balance, with a strong leadership, although he never shared Mascagni's unwavering support for 'Il Duce'.

By now Puccini was fast losing faith in *Turandot* and most particularly in his ability to finish the job. He briefly toyed with the notion of returning to the original two-act formula as he couldn't face the idea of having to work on two further acts, and felt so lacking in hope by the end of the year that he was all for giving up the project. The first few months of 1923 saw him composing as if drawing teeth. Feelings of creative burn-out haunted him continually, and even when the music flowed tolerably well he felt tired of the relentless cycle of operatic creation which had been his compositional treadmill for most of his working life.

Nevertheless, April saw most of the second act completed, and in the following month a fruitful discussion regarding a number of problems he was having with the libretto of Act III led to everything being ironed out to his satisfaction. His spirits were also raised considerably by a visit to Vienna to see the premiere there of *Manon Lescaut*. According to a letter of the time he was wined, dined and celebrated as though he were 'the Kaiser'. He did, however, have to spend several days at a local clinic undergoing treatment for his diabetes, using insulin – then a novel procedure. He still found time for a hunting trip to Torre del Lago and purchased a new motor boat capable of speeds in excess of twenty-five miles an hour, but otherwise the remainder of the year was spent working on *Turandot*.

Typically, as he began the third act and had therefore the end in sight, Puccini's mood lightened to the extent that he now believed his previous work to be insignificant in comparison. By February 1924 he was nearly there and was already anticipating the gala premiere planned for April 1925 at La Scala, with Beniamino Gigli as Calaf and Toscanini on the conductor's podium (Puccini had begun to restore some of his former good relations with the maestro).

While work continued on *Turandot*, there was musical diversion of a different kind: Puccini attended the Italian premiere of Schoenberg's *Pierrot lunaire* in Florence on 1 April, and then exactly a month later the world premiere of Boito's *Nerone*, which had been left incomplete at the composer's death in 1918. Tellingly, it was Schoenberg's work that really fired Puccini's enthusiasm (Schoenberg was also an admirer of Puccini); *Nerone*, after much hype and bluster, turned out to be something of a failure. Interestingly, Puccini referred to himself as having a 'nerone' streak insofar as he tended to relish depicting any on-stage nastiness, most memorably the beheading of the Prince in the first act of *Turandot*.

Of more concern was the soreness in Puccini's throat which had become increasingly wearisome since March. A visit to a spa in May and several specialist diagnoses brought no discernible improvement – which perhaps was hardly surprising when rheumatism was suggested as the root cause. Writing to Sybil, Puccini complained, 'My throat is just the same – the cure hasn't made any difference. They say that I shall feel better later – we'll see.' Finally a Florentine specialist discovered a tumour and, although he made reassuring noises to Puccini about the outcome, to the composer's son Tonio he confessed that he considered it inoperable.

During September Puccini was visited by Toscanini who was keen to see how work on *Turandot* was progressing. It seems that by now all differences over the war had been resolved or forgotten and the two were friends once more. 'We are in perfect agreement and I breathe at last,' Puccini reported to Adami. 'The little that I played to Toscanini made an excellent impression.' However, the following month the composer was clearly going downhill fast:

I am going through a terrible time. This trouble in my throat is giving me no rest, although the torment is more mental than physical. I am going to Brussels to consult a well-known specialist... Will it be an operation? Or medical treatment? Or sentence of death? I cannot go on any longer like this.

The seriousness of his situation was kept from Puccini, even when in November he headed for Brussels where a new development in radium treatment offered a faint glimmer of hope. A letter to a close friend back in Viareggio reveals the degree of torment he was suffering:

I am crucified like Christ. I have a collar round my throat which is like some form of torture. External X-ray treatment at present – then crystal needles into my throat and a hole in order to breathe, this too in my neck... In the mornings I spit mouthfuls of dark blood. But the doctor says this is nothing serious... We'll see.

On 24 November Puccini underwent a surgical operation under local anaesthetic as his diabetes posed too great a risk for him to have a general. The operation itself was a success, and for a while it looked as though Puccini might pull through; but on the morning of 29 November his heart gave out under the strain. He was sixty-five years old. Elvira had been too ill to make the journey to be at his bedside, although one of the last things Puccini said to his step-daughter Fosca was, 'Remember, your mother is a remarkable woman'. At the end he was unable to speak at all and had to write everything down. His last inscription reads: 'Elvira, povera donna, e finito' ('Elvira, poor woman, it's over'). Elvira even missed the funeral service on 3 December; it was given the status of a national event, with Toscanini conducting the

Puccini's funeral in Brussels, as represented by R. Salvadori for the cover of the weekly newspaper
La Domenica del Corriere

funeral music from Act III of *Edgar*. Initially the body was laid in the Toscanini family tomb, but two years later Elvira arranged for it to be moved to a private chapel in Torre del Lago, where she too now lies buried.

Tantalisingly, *Turandot* was virtually complete, with just twenty-two pages of sketches remaining that would normally have been expanded to finish the opera, starting from the scene after Liù's death. The job of completing the work fell to Franco Alfano, the fifty-year-old composer of *Sakuntala* (1921), an oriental extravaganza that demonstrated an intuitive command of Eastern idioms. Initially he produced 377 bars of music, although Toscanini considered this first version to contain too much of Alfano and requested a shorter solution that eventually ran to just 268 bars.

During the eventual premiere of *Turandot*, on 25 April 1926 at La Scala, Toscanini lowered his baton just after the death of Liù and turned to the audience with barely contained emotion to announce that this was the point at which Puccini had laid his creative pen to rest for the very last time. On what was already a highly charged occasion, this opened up the floodgates and the audience was reportedly reduced to emotional rubble. For the remaining performances of the run, the work was performed with Alfano's abbreviated ending, which is the one almost invariably played to this day.

Turandot scored a resounding success and has remained one of the few twentieth-century operas to have sustained a firm foothold in opera houses throughout the world. Far from being a burnt-out ember of late Romanticism, it reveals that Puccini's exposure to Stravinsky and Schoenberg was at last bearing musical fruit. Having shied away from grand opera virtually all his composing life, in *Turandot* he shows an acute mastery of the epic of which even he barely thought himself capable. In many ways the work brought him full circle from his orchestral beginnings. Whenever Puccini had used operatic precedents for grandeur and spectacle (principally Verdi and Meyerbeer) the results were almost invariably unconvincing and impersonal. It was through the French, Russian and German orchestral traditions that he at last found a way of remaining utterly true to himself, but on a much-expanded scale.

One significant example of Puccini's new approach occurs in the second act at Turandot's 'In questa reggia' ('Within this palace'). Quite apart from the expansive tessitura from a low C sharp/D flat to a high C natural, Puccini indulges in all manner of wide leaps and jagged intervals which chillingly enhance this paean against Love. In the passage in which Turandot announces that she will never be possessed by a man, no fewer than five times does Puccini have the soprano encompass the descent of a 9th, possibly a reflection of the intervallic leaps and bounds of Schoenberg's *Pierrot lunaire*, which he so admired. It remains one of the most gruelling passages in the whole operatic repertoire, especially as Turandot must sing flat out for much of the time and is often expected to rise above a large orchestra playing at full force. Even after this, Turandot has to muster her energies for the powerful exchanges with Calaf regarding the three riddles. Turandot is no anti-heroic cipher but a living, breathing being whose inexorable, icy touch is thrillingly suggested by Puccini's off-the-leash portrait of degradation.

Puccini achieves a moving contrast between Turandot's near-hysteria and Liù's delicate composure and touching nobility. If Turandot is ultimately transfigured by feelings of love, it is Liù's destiny that to love is to die. Puccini's writing for her is much closer to his customary style. Her two main arias – 'Signore, ascolta!' ('My lord, listen to me') and 'Tu, che di gel sei cinta' ('You are wrapped in ice') – show his

Turandot

Act I: The walls of Peking in ancient times. People are swarming around as a Mandarin makes a public declaration: Princess Turandot will marry anyone of royal blood if he succeeds in solving three riddles; if he fails, he dies. The Prince of Persia is the latest suitor to have failed in his quest and is to be beheaded at moonrise. The people crowd around, eager to get a decent view of the execution, but are forced back by the imperial guards. Among the seething crowd is Timur, the deposed and blind Tartar king, aided by his devoted Chinese slave girl, Liù. When Timur falls to the ground Liù appeals for assistance; recognising his father, Prince Calaf steps forward to assist. He asks Liù why she has remained so faithful and she replies that it was because he, the Prince, once smiled on her.

The crowd bays for blood but when the people see the young Persian Prince making his tired but dignified way to the block, they cry out for clemency. Turandot now appears, her radiant beauty immediately capturing Calaf's heart. Yet behind her striking exterior beats an icy heart and with barely a flicker of emotion she indicates that the execution should go ahead. Even as the cries of the Prince are heard in the distance all Calaf can think about is Turandot. Despite pleas by Timur and Liù, and warnings from the Emperor's three ministers Ping, Pang and Pong, Calaf strikes the ceremonial gong that signifies the arrival of a new suitor.

Act II: Ping, Pang and Pong are in their living quarters in a palace pavilion. They reflect on the violence of Turandot's reign and recall the twenty-seven suitors who have already given their lives in pursuit of her love. They are shaken from their reverie by the sound of drums and trumpets that usher in the second scene, set in a square in front of the imperial palace. The Emperor Altoum is on a high throne, attended by the eight wise men who carry the scrolls on which are inscribed the answers to the various riddles. He also tries to dissuade Calaf from taking the path to almost certain destruction, yet the Prince remains firm.

Turandot enters and relates the story of her ancestor Lou-Ling who was brutally murdered by a visiting prince. As a result Turandot has vowed that she will never be possessed by a man. She poses the first of three riddles: 'What is born anew every night but dies at dawn?' 'La speranza' ('hope'), comes the correct response. Turandot, unmoved, moves on to her second question: 'What flickers red like a flame, yet is not a flame?' 'Il sangue' ('blood'), the Prince responds correctly. By now shaken, Turandot reaches the third and final riddle: 'What is like ice but burns?' There is an electrifying silence until Calaf cries out triumphantly, 'Turandot!' The Princess tries to panic her father into not giving her away to the Prince, who in response generously puts forward a puzzle of his own: if Turandot can discover his real name before dawn she will be released from the contract and be free to execute him.

Act III: The gardens of the palace. Just before dawn, Turandot hysterically announces that if the Prince's name isn't discovered she will execute everyone. It is at this point that the Prince sings what has become the most famous of all tenor arias, 'Nessun dorma'. In desperation Ping, Pang and Pong plead with him, whereupon the people threaten to get the information out of Timur and Liù. Turandot emerges on the scene and orders Liù's torture. She remains silent and when asked by Turandot how she has withstood the torture she replies that it was through 'Love'. In a fit of pique Turandot orders the torture to be intensified, whereupon Liù swiftly removes a dagger from a guard's belt and stabs herself, falling dead at Timur's feet. The company carries the body away, leaving Turandot and Calaf alone. Calaf rushes across to Turandot and kisses her passionately. For the first time in her life the icy Princess experiences feelings of physical tenderness. Having at last won the Princess's heart Calaf reveals his name. In the short final scene Turandot reveals the stranger's name to the Emperor and the eager, thronging crowd – 'it is Love'.

imagination working at full stretch as he intermingles and ultimately resolves the pentatonic idioms of the East with the harmonic opulence of the West. Liù's final scene includes her impassioned 'L'amore?', as she explains what drove her to withstand torture. Here Puccini combines the self-effacing purity of Cio-Cio-San with Tosca's indomitability, expressed with a new and tantalising emotional economy. Timur's dignified reaction to Liù's dramatic suicide ('Liù… bontà') is cast not as an outburst of Rodolfo-like hysteria but as emotionally numbed recitative, as though Timur is at first incapable of melodic thought.

Puccini's propensity for confessing his own shortcomings through his operatic characters also reaches its apogee in the final pages of the first act, in which Calaf's empty reassurances that Liù's patience will ultimately be rewarded ('Non piangere, Liù!') mirrors Puccini's own dealings with Elvira. Timur's attempts to dissuade Calaf from trying to conquer the Princess ('Ah! Per l'ultima volta') may also be interpreted as symbolising those friends (most notably Giulio Ricordi) who down the years had wagged fingers of sanctimonious disapproval at Puccini's string of sexual peccadilloes.

Another important aspect of *Turandot* is Puccini's use of the chorus. Almost like a Greek tragedy it plays an active role in events and comments upon them in the manner of Mussorgsky's *Boris Godunov*. This was unprecedented not only in Puccini's work but in Italian opera as a whole. As with *Madama Butterfly*, Puccini used a number of authentic melodies, some of which were picked up from Chinese musical boxes owned by an acquaintance. (One of them still survives and unmistakably suggests a snatch of melody that is associated with Turandot throughout the opera.) Unlike in *Madama Butterfly*, however, the melodies are used less for local colour than as a vital and imposing part of the musical fabric. This is further enhanced by Puccini's exotic scoring, which includes an array of added percussion, including gong. The dissonant music and use of exotic percussion found at the Court of the Chinese Emperor in Stravinsky's *Le Rossignol* ('The Nightingale', 1914) might have provided a model for Puccini's work on *Turandot*.

Again to the fore is Puccini's mastery of collage effects and characterisation, so that during the first act in particular, over and above the usual intricate web of signature motifs symbolising individual characters and moods, he finds contrasting sound worlds for each role or group; they appear to flow smoothly into each other like ripples in a stream.

The premiere of *Turandot* was nearly derailed by a showdown between Mussolini and Toscanini. The conductor had stood firm against a decree that the theatre should display pictures of the King and Il Duce; he had also withstood pressure to perform the *Giovanezza*, a Fascist rallying song, at performances. Discovering that Mussolini was due to visit Milan for Empire Day celebrations, it was felt expedient to issue an invitation to the première; Mussolini agreed on condition that the *Giovanezza* was performed. Toscanini adamantly refused, and, as Mosco Carner puts it, 'there was no *Giovanezza* and no Duce to mar the baptism of Puccini's swansong'. So the premiere was able to take place free from political distractions, and the reaction of public and press was mainly enthusiastic. The *Corriere della sera* report stated:

> [Turandot] *is produced by a dominant personality of great experience with an acute sense of theatre which gives yet another proof of the versatility of the Maestro in adapting with his brilliance as a colourist all the less typical exotic musical elements into a modern art form.*

The lure of exoticism, the strength of the plot, the presence of the iconic aria 'Nessun dorma' ('None shall sleep'), and the attractions of the principal roles for performers and audiences alike – all these are factors calculated to keep the opera as a permanent fixture in opera houses round the world. As regards *Turandot*'s place in operatic history, the scholar Jürgen Maehder asserts that it represented a synthesis of diverse European traditions:

> It is a fully mature opera not only in terms of Puccini's own output, but also as the last descendant of the Italian operatic tradition of the nineteenth century, and it reflects in both its dramaturgy and its music the ideas that were currently sweeping across Europe.

Epilogue

With Puccini's passing, the grand tradition of Italian Romantic opera came to an end. There was no one remotely capable of inheriting his mantle, and the onslaught of modernism made it increasingly unfashionable for anyone to emulate the kind of expressive intensity that audiences could assimilate on first hearing. The very foundations on which Italian opera had originally been based – its emotional directness and simplicity – were now history. And the critic Fausto Torrefranca had not been alone in seeking to condemn the hegemony of opera in Italy; young composers who came after Puccini were perhaps grateful not to have been shackled to a distinguished but now outmoded performing tradition, and one which would have problems in adapting itself not only to changes in the make-up of society, but also to the latest trends in composition.

Yet Puccini's music went on to exert a profound influence on several new musical genres then in their infancy. The first 'talkies' emerged shortly after Puccini's death and film music consequently owed a tremendous debt of gratitude to his dramatic techniques. There is even a case to be made that Puccini's work was temperamentally and stylistically closer to, say, Miklós Rózsa's epic music for *Ben-Hur* (1959) than to operas such as Verdi's *La traviata*.

The emergence of music theatre and later the Broadway and Hollywood musical was made possible by Puccini's supreme example of making words and music indissoluble. Above all, Puccini's unrivalled ear for heart-stopping melody set a blueprint for tin-pan alley songsters and the crooner tradition from Bing Crosby and Frank Sinatra to Vic Damone and Michael Bublé. If Puccini's impact on mainstream twentieth-century classical music was minimal, on popular idioms it was incalculable. In one sense his music was a glorious sunset, yet in another it was a bracing new dawn.

Personalities

Adami, Giuseppe (1878–1946): Italian journalist and playwright. He wrote the librettos for *La rondine, Il tabarro* and *Turandot* (with Renato Simoni). He later published biographies of both Puccini and Giulio Ricordi.

Alfano, Franco (1875–1954): Italian composer and pianist. He composed a large number of piano and orchestral pieces as well as several operas (including *Cyrano de Bergerac*), but is now principally remembered for his completion of *Turandot*.

Bazzini, Antonio (1818–1897): Italian composer, violinist and teacher. He spent the early part of his career touring as a virtuoso violinist before settling in Italy in 1863, where he attempted to establish an instrumental tradition. His pupils included Puccini, Mascagni and Catalani.

Belasco, David (1854–1931): American playwright, director and theatrical producer. He was involved in over 100 Broadway productions and his works inspired some forty movies. His greatest claim to fame is as the writer of *Madame Butterfly* and *The Golden Girl of the West.*

Boito, Arrigo (1842–1918): Italian poet, journalist, novelist and composer. He was responsible for a number of celebrated opera librettos, including Verdi's *Falstaff* and *Otello*. His most famous self-penned opera is *Mefistofele*.

Carignani, Carlo (1857–1919): Italian composer, conductor and vocal trainer. He studied alongside Puccini at the Pacini Institute in Lucca and went on to transcribe nearly all his operas as piano and vocal scores.

Caruso, Enrico (1873–1921): Italian tenor. He became a legend in his own lifetime, making over 260 recordings and achieving great wealth in the process. He created the role of Dick Johnson in *La fanciulla del West*.

Catalani, Alfredo (1854–1893): Italian composer of fastidious taste. Now principally remembered for the last of his five operas, *La Wally*, he deeply resented Giulio Ricordi for supporting Puccini in preference to himself.

Civinini, Guelfo (1873–1954): Italian journalist and poet. He collaborated with Carlo Zangarini on the libretto of *La fanciulla del West*, although he later found his true métier as a travel writer.

D'Annunzio, Gabriele (1863–1938): Italian poet, journalist, novelist, dramatist, and mentor to Mussolini. He made various unsuccessful attempts to collaborate with Puccini on an opera.

Dalla Rizza, Gilda (1892–1975): Italian soprano. Celebrated for her remarkable range and versatility, she created the role of Magda in *La rondine* and was Puccini's ideal Minnie in *La fanciulla del West*.

Del Fiorentino, Dante (1888–?): Italian priest. He first met Puccini in 1903 after the composer's automobile accident; he emigrated to America and in 1951 published some reminiscences of their various times together.

Fontana, Ferdinando (1850–1919): Italian poet, playwright and librettist. He provided the librettos for both *Le villi* and *Edgar*, and first brought *Manon Lescaut* and *Tosca* to Puccini's attention.

Forzano, Giovacchino (1884–1970): Italian playwright, editor, producer, and the writer of over fifty librettos including Puccini's *Suor Angelica* and *Gianni Schicchi*.

Franchetti, Alberto (1860–1942): Italian composer of noble birth often referred to as the 'Meyerbeer of Italy' due to his love of the epic scenario. His most celebrated collaboration was with Puccini on *Tosca*.

Gemignani, Fosca (1880–1968): Daughter of Narcisco Gemignani and Elvira. She accompanied her mother on her extended elopement with Puccini, later becoming the composer's stepdaughter.

Giacosa, Giuseppe (1847–1906): Italian poet, playwright and librettist and one of the most distinguished literary figures of his generation. He collaborated with Luigi Illica as verse poet on Puccini's three most celebrated operas: *La Bohème*, *Tosca* and *Madama Butterfly*.

Gold, Didier (dates unknown): French playwright. His most famous creation, *La Houppelande* ('The Cloak'), formed the basis of *Il tabarro*.

Illica, Luigi (1857–1919): Italian playwright and librettist who lost his right ear in a duel over a woman. He collaborated with Giuseppe Giacosa as scenario librettist on *La Bohème*, *Tosca* and *Madama Butterfly*.

Leoncavallo, Ruggero (1857–1919): Italian composer whose most famous opera, *I pagliacci*, was composed in direct response to Mascagni's *Cavalleria rusticana*. He briefly worked on the libretto of *Manon Lescaut*.

Magi, Fortunato (1839–1882): Italian composer, conductor, teacher and Puccini's uncle on his mother's side. He gave young Giacomo his first organ and singing lessons.

Mascagni, Pietro (1863–1945): Italian composer principally remembered for his defining, one-act *verismo* opera *Cavalleria rusticana*. He and Puccini remained good friends despite periods of healthy professional rivalry.

Mugnone, Leopoldo (1858–1941): Italian conductor and composer. He conducted the premieres of *Tosca* and the revised version of *Edgar*. His most popular work was the operetta *Il birichino*.

Oliva, Domenico (1860–1917): Italian poet who was one of six writers to be involved in the libretto of *Manon Lescaut*. His work on the final act remained fairly intact throughout all subsequent revisions.

Ponchielli, Amilcare (1834–1886): Italian composer and teacher famous for the opera *La Gioconda*. One of Puccini's earliest champions, he succeeded in involving Fontana as librettist for *Le villi*.

Praga, Marco (1862–1929): Distinguished Italian playwright who enjoyed a brief flirtation with the libretto for *Manon Lescaut*.

Puccini, Albina (1830–1884): Puccini's mother. She was an unending tower of strength and support, especially following the death of Puccini's father in 1864.

Puccini, Antonio ('Tonio') (1885–1946): Puccini and Elvira's son. He studied engineering, thus ending the family's centuries-old musical tradition.

Puccini, Elvira (*née* Bonturi) (1860–1930): Puccini's wife; earlier the wife of Narciso Gemignani. In 1885 she eloped with Puccini and shortly afterwards gave birth to their son Tonio. Narciso died in 1903, leaving Puccini and Elvira free to marry at last.

Puccini, Michele senior (1813–1864): Italian composer and organist, and Puccini's father. He was a widely respected and consulted authority on sacred music and theory, while sustaining the family's musical tradition as organist of the Cathedral of San Martino.

Puccini, Michele junior (1864–1891): Puccini's younger brother, born three months after their father's death. After being trained as a musician at the Milan Conservatoire he emigrated to South America where, following a series of adventures, he died from yellow fever.

Ricordi, Giulio (1840–1912): Italian music publisher, representing the third generation of the family firm. Giulio was the man who first nurtured Puccini's talent for opera and continued to support him through even the blackest of creative periods.

Ricordi, Tito (1865–1933): Italian music publisher and son of Giulio Ricordi. He took over the firm following his father's death in 1912. Although (with the exception of *La rondine*) Puccini continued to publish his music with Ricordi, there was a decided cooling-off in relations.

Sardou, Victorien (1831–1908): French dramatist. His most famous work was *La Tosca*, which was written specifically for Sarah Bernhardt and later adapted by Puccini to become a *verismo* operatic sensation.

Seligman, Sybil (1868–1935): English wife of David Seligman, a wealthy London banker, and society hostess whose artistic sensibilities were a profound source of inspiration and succour for Puccini following their first encounter in 1904.

Sonzogno, Edoardo (1836–1920): Italian music publisher and principal rival of Ricordi. Sonzogno's roster of composers included Mascagni, Leoncavallo, Cilea and Giordano.

Sonzogno, Lorenzo (1877–1920): Italian music publisher and nephew of Edoardo. He was responsible for picking up Puccini's *La rondine* on the rebound from Ricordi.

Toscanini, Arturo (1867–1957): Italian conductor. His scorching interpretations were without rival. He conducted the premieres of *La Bohème*, *La fanciulla del West* and *Turandot*.

Tosti, Sir Francesco Paolo (1846–1916): Italian composer of popular songs and teacher. His pupils included royalty and London's rich and famous; one of them, Sybil Seligman, he introduced to Puccini.

Zangarini, Carlo (1874–1943): Italian poet and librettist. He joined forces with Guelfo Civinini on the libretto of *La fanciulla del West*.

Selected Bibliography

Ashbrook, William, *The Operas of Puccini*, New York, 1968

Budden, Julian, *Puccini: His Life and Works*, Oxford, 2002

Carner, Mosco, ed., *Letters of Puccini*, London, 1974

Carner, Mosco, *Puccini: A Critical Biography*, London, 1958

Girardi, Michele, *Puccini: His International Art*, Chicago, 2000

Greenfield, Edward, *Puccini, Keeper of the Seal*, London, 1958

Greenfield, Howard, *Puccini: A Biography*, London, 1981

Marek, George R., *Puccini*, New York, 1951

Osborne, Charles, *The Complete Operas of Puccini*, New York, 1982

Phillips-Matz, Mary Jane, *Puccini: A Biography*, Boston, 2002

Sadie, Stanley, ed., *Puccini and His Operas*, London, 2000

Seligman, Vincent, *Puccini among Friends*, London, 1938

Weaver, William, *Puccini: The Man and his Music*, New York, 1977

Wilson, Conrad, *Giacomo Puccini*, London 1997

Glossary

Appoggiatura A leaning or suspended note that often heightens emotional intensity by delaying the arrival of its downward resolution.

Aria An extended solo passage in an opera or oratorio.

Bel canto Literally 'fine singing'. A vocal style, especially associated with Bellini, that emphasises long, flowing lines.

Cantabile 'In a singing style' – a performance direction to play or sing in a melodious, flowing manner.

Cantata A work in several movements for accompanied voice or voices (from the Latin *cantare*, to sing).

Capriccio A caprice; a work (usually in free form) structured according to the whim of the composer.

Cavatina Operatic solo aria (or instrumental piece) of a flowing, song-like nature.

Chromaticism/ chromatic The use of notes foreign to the scale of the main key. On a piano keyboard C major uses only the white keys, therefore making all the black ones in between 'chromatic'.

Compound time The division of the beats into a set of three – typified by time signatures such as 6/8 and 9/8. It is ideal for imparting a sense of easy, conversational flow or a skipping lilt.

Counterpoint/ contrapuntal A style of writing in which two or more independent parts (voices) are performed at the same time.

Crescendo Getting gradually louder.

Dissonance A chord which is jarring to the ear. In Puccini's music this is invariably at a low level and caused by the presence of a note or notes foreign to a chord to create a dramatic effect.

Duet A composition or part thereof written for two soloists, accompanied or unaccompanied.

Elegy A musical lament, often for the dead.

Fugue/fugal A work or part of a work which is based on imitative counterpoint, with voices answering each other in different keys, in inversion etc.

Harmony Everything that pertains to the vertical aspect of music, most especially chords, their types and behaviour.

Intermezzo In Puccini's operas, an orchestral interlude inserted into an opera, usually denoting the passage of time.

Key The gravitational 'tonality' of a piece of music towards which all other keys relate or ultimately resolve.

Leitmotif A short recurring musical phrase or motif in an opera used to denote a person, object, emotion or concept.

Libretto The written text of an opera or other extended vocal work.

Madrigal Vocal composition for several (usually unaccompanied) voices, first developed in the thirteenth century and gradually superseded by the cantata during the seventeenth century.

Mass Christian religious service, from the Latin *missa*. The Ordinary of the Mass included those parts of the Mass text that did not vary with the occasion: Kyrie (Lord have mercy), Gloria (Glory to God in the highest), Credo (I believe), Sanctus – Benedictus (Holy, Holy – Blessed) and Agnus Dei (O Lamb of God).

Melody Everything that pertains to the horizontal aspect of music, most especially a sustained single line.

Minuet Instrumental dance in triple time especially popular during the eighteenth century.

Modes The names given to the particular arrangement of notes within a scale. The commonest modes are those that we call major and minor. The church modes prevalent in the Middle Ages differed depending on the sequence of tones and semitones. Since the early eighteenth century these have generally only been used to create some kind of archaic effect. Puccini sometimes used these modes to blur and therefore suspend the sensation of being in a particular key.

Motet A form of short unaccompanied vocal composition, invariably sacred in nature, especially prevalent from the sixteenth century. Motets may be introduced into a service at the Offertory, during the Elevation of the Host and at other times when the liturgy does not prescribe a particular text to be sung.

Opera buffa Comic opera. As well as humour, *opera buffa* was characterised by a flexibility in form and a broader scope of subject.

Opera seria Literally 'serious opera'. Highly formalised and mainly based on mythological subjects.

Orchestration The way in which a composer or arranger distributes a piece of music among the various members or sections of an orchestra or band.

Overture Piece of instrumental music intended to introduce an opera, oratorio, play or ballet. There are also many well-known examples of overtures written as concert works.

Parallel 4ths/ 5ths The intervals of a 4th or 5th in music harmony are known as 'perfect' intervals. To western ears they possess an 'open' quality and when sounded consecutively (in parallel) are suggestive (depending on the context) of medieval monastic chanting or the Orient.

Pedal point(s) A sustained note or notes in the bass line held below changing harmonies above. If the sustained note appears in a higher register it is known as an inverted pedal.

Phrase A group of notes that embrace a distinct unit of musical expression, normally singable in one breath.

Pizzicato Plucked strings.

Prelude An orchestral preface designed to establish the mood of either an entire work or act. There are also many examples of free-standing instrumental preludes.

Recitative Originally a formal narrative section of a vocal work designed to impart information, typically accompanied by harpsichord. By Puccini's time it had become little more than a passing device subsumed into the music's onward flow.

Requiem Mass for the Dead which broadly follows the words of the Catholic Mass, but with the celebratory sections (Gloria and Credo) omitted, and the Dies Irae (Day of Wrath) inserted.

Scale From the Italian *scala* ('ladder') indicating a series of normally adjacent notes moving up or down in step. Major and minor scales divide the octave into a series of tones and semitones. To evoke mystery Puccini occasionally employed the whole-tone scale, in which each step is a whole tone. For a suggestion of the Orient, he used the pentatonic or five-note scale, the intervals of which are as the black keys on the piano.

Scherzo/ scherzando Literally a 'joke', the scherzo (or even lighter scherzando) originated as a lively offshoot of the relatively formal lines of the minuet. Following Mendelssohn's example, it is most often associated with 'will-o'-the-wisp' speed and delicacy.

Score The vertical arrangement in notation of all the vocal and instrumental parts of a work enabling a conductor or reader to see every part at any given moment.

Staccato Detached articulation, the opposite of legato.

String quartet A chamber ensemble consisting of two violins, viola and cello; also the name given to works written for that combination, typically in three or four movements.

Suspension A note from one chord held over into a following chord of which it is not a member. The result is invariably a heightening of emotional intensity.

Symphony/ symphonic An orchestral work, typically in three or four contrasting movements, usually exhibiting a high level of creative vigour and ingenuity. For Italians of the nineteenth century, 'symphonic' denoted virtually anything that was more complex than the 'rum-ti-tum' of standard operatic accompaniments.

Syncopation/ syncopated A type of rhythm in which the emphasised notes fall between the music's natural strong beats.

Tremolando/ tremolo From the Italian for 'trembling' or 'shaking', a dramatic effect created by either the fast repetition of a single note (typically by string instruments) or the rapid oscillation of two notes (typically on a keyboard).

Verismo A movement in Italian opera towards the end of the nineteenth century dedicated to gritty 'realism', particularly in the depiction of grim or sordid events.

Waltz A dance in triple time that became universally popular during the nineteenth century, most associated with the Strauss family of Vienna.

Annotations of CD Tracks

Works marked ⓦ may be heard in full by logging onto the website (see page i).

CD 1

ⓦ Messa di gloria (Messa a quattro voci)
1 VII: Credo in unum Deum
2 VIII: Et incarnatus est

Composed in 1880 as Puccini's graduation piece from the Pacini Institute in Lucca, the *Messa di gloria* (more correctly the *Messa a quattro voci*) incorporates two existing pieces. One is the 1878 Credo ('I believe in one God'), a searingly dramatic piece in C minor somewhat at odds with the majesty normally associated with this part of the Mass. If the music's expressive changeability – hushed vocal lines are splintered by orchestral shafts of light – owes something to Verdi's Requiem (written only four years earlier), Puccini's occasional delight in two-against-three cross-rhythms suggests an awareness of Brahms's *Deutsches Requiem* (1868). Most notable of all is the wide-ranging arch of the main theme and the imposing orchestral writing. The Credo flows directly into the soothing G major 'Et incarnatus est' ('And he was made incarnate'), which features a plaintive tenor solo of Gounod-like fervour, indicating that Puccini was probably familiar with the great Frenchman's church music.

3 Preludio sinfonico

Two years after the *Messa a quattro voci*, while still a student at the Milan Conservatoire, Puccini composed the *Preludio sinfonico* in A major. Its obvious model is Wagner's *Lohengrin*, although the string writing also owes something to the slow movement of Mendelssohn's 'Scottish' Symphony. In the more heated central section (with its rather inflated grand climax) the octave doublings in the upper strings anticipate a technique Puccini would employ in his later operas. This is the first piece in which one senses him moving above and beyond the generic borrowings of his earlier music and relishing a new command of orchestral texture, thanks in no small part to his lessons with Bazzini.

Le villi

4 Act I: Prelude

5 Act I: Se come voi piccina io fossì

6 Act II: La tregenda (Witches' Dance)

Puccini's first opera opens atmospherically, leading the audience gently into the first scene via a series of musical premonitions of the work to come. The perky woodwind opening, although enchanting, is not particularly suggestive of its composer, but Puccini's voice is unmistakable as soon as the strings sweep in. The leaning intervallic fall of a 2nd, mirrored by its upward inversion, is a musical metaphor for swooning that is unmistakably Puccinian. The music has only just started, yet already we feel emotionally transported.

At the orchestral opening of Anna's Act I aria 'Se come voi piccina io fossì, o vaghi fior' ('If I were like you, pretty flowers') one could almost be listening to *Madama Butterfly*, so distinctive is Puccini's orchestration and musical patterning. There is nothing in Verdi's orchestral palette (nor Wagner's for that matter) to compare with the magical sounds Puccini creates with his pedal-pointed modal harmonies and distinctive combination of piccolo, glockenspiel, harp, cymbals and shimmering strings. The way in which Anna's vocal line steals in is emblematic, its constant ebb and flow of rising and falling scalic figurations dropping gently back only to start again, but this time rising even higher. Note also the constant chains of suspending appoggiaturas involving Puccini's favourite drop of a major 2nd, and how the strings intensify the swelling of emotion by climbing upwards from underneath when the vocal line relaxes downwards. The following verse, in which Anna sings 'You flowers who are more fortunate than I, will follow my beloved over hills and dales', is especially touching and provides the blueprint of glowing innocence for Mimì in *La Bohème*, the music's freshness and candour enhanced by its emancipation from Wagnerian chromaticisms.

Although 'La tregenda', which sets up the action of Act II, is more stylistically generalised, with its echoes of Italian opera-ballet music in the tradition of *Aida* and with a Bizet-like glitter and panache, the music's rhythmic thrust and sheer ebullience carry it along. Most significant is a breezy contentedness, created by a harmonic suspension over an inverted pedal point, underpinned by a skipping bass line, and by Puccini's characteristic delight in juxtaposing emotional opposites, as witness the opening few bars.

7 Edgar. Act III: Prelude

This brief Prelude, chosen by Toscanini to be performed at Puccini's funeral, is acknowledged as the most inspired of the music in *Edgar*. It manages to encapsulate in just three and a half minutes the solemnity and sadness of the fake funeral at the act's beginning, with only the grandiose ending breaking the music's undeniable spell.

The libretto describes in detail the scene that Puccini so memorably evokes here: 'The bastion of a fortress near the city of Courtray. The sun is setting and black clouds mingle in the falling sky. The funeral procession files past, the coffin bearing a dead knight in armour. Laurel leaves are strewn over the coffin. Frank appears with a Friar, his face concealed by his habit. Fidelio, Gualtiero and soldiers watch as the coffin is lowered into the catafalque.'

8 Crisantemi (version for string orchestra)

Crisantemi is a brooding elegy, composed between *Edgar* and *Manon Lescaut* and cast in A–B–A form, in which the music of the two outer sections is contrasted with a different theme over a pedal point in the middle. It represents the summit of Puccini's admiration for Wagner's music, the opening few bars, with soprano and bass lines tugging in opposite directions, sounding almost as if it could have come straight from *Tristan und Isolde*. Puccini reused some of the material in the final act of *Manon Lescaut*, where its heady brew of chromatic harmonies and suspensions adds considerably to the louring atmosphere. Originally written for string quartet, its strongly perfumed, chromatically saturated yearnings possess a heightened sensuality more redolent of the concert hall than the chamber room; they gain considerably from the textural cushioning and velvety warmth of multiple strings.

(w) Manon Lescaut

9 Act I: Donna non vidi mai simile a questa!

10 Act II: In quelle trine morbide

11 Act III: Intermezzo

12 Act IV: Sola, perduta, abbandonata

The distance that Puccini travelled between *Edgar* and *Manon Lescaut* can immediately be sensed from Des Grieux's Act I aria 'Donna non vidi', in which he describes the overwhelming effect that Manon has had on him. 'I've never before seen such a woman!' he sings. 'To say to her "I love you" awakens a new inspiration in my soul. "My name is Manon Lescaut". How those fragrant words inflame my spirit, and every part of me wants to caress her. May the gentle whispers never cease!' This is an early example of a technique that Puccini would use frequently in his soaring solo numbers: the violins intensify the vocal line by playing with it in unison, while also filling in or tracing around it so as to create the impression of an inter-weaving counter-melody. Notice also how the violins drop away when the mood relaxes slightly, particularly in the lower register.

By the time Manon sings her Act II aria 'In quelle trine morbide' she has gone where the money is: with Geronte. Despite having achieved all the trappings of wealth she feels thoroughly empty inside. 'In these soft silken drapes and gilded alcoves, there's a cold and deadly silence,' she confesses, 'a coldness that freezes me! Then I had fervent caresses and sensual kisses from ardent lips, but now I have something totally different! I think about my humble dwelling, happy, secluded and white; like a gentle dream of peace and love.' Puccini's doubling of the vocal line is more varied here, with the higher register mirrored at the same pitch, the lower register doubled an octave lower. As the music briefly relaxes, so the doubling stops and the woodwind briefly take over.

Both the preceding arias are strongly premonitory of *La Bohème*'s lyrical surge, yet the Act III Intermezzo, for all its haunting evocation of desolation and loneliness as it describes Manon's journey to Le Havre and the awaiting prison boat, opens with a passage whose indebtedness to Wagner is, like *Crisantemi*, so overt that Puccini's creative voice becomes momentarily hidden from view. As the music changes to a more Italianate lyricism at 1:22, it is almost as though Puccini has suddenly woken up following a brief Bayreuth reverie. This aria-without-words is also one of Puccini's most overtly Tchaikovskyan passages, the emotional pressure being increased incrementally by the repetition of short-breathed phrases, driven higher and higher towards a fever-pitch climax that then falls back exhausted.

One of Puccini's strengths was his ability to suggest impending doom and tragedy, and even if Manon's crushing despair in 'Sola, perduta, abbandonata' briefly becomes the kind of hysterical emotional bludgeoning that Puccini avoided in later life, it is still a scene of extraordinary power. 'Alone, lost and forsaken in this desolate land. What a horror! The sky darkens around me,' Manon despairs. 'I die in the depths of the desert, a cruel torture, alone and forsaken. I don't want to die! It's all over for me!'

w La Bohème

13 Act I: Che gelida manina
14 Act I: Mi chiamano Mimì
15 Act II: Quando me'n vo'
16 Act II: Ahi! Che c'è?
17 Act IV: Sono andati?
18 Act IV: La mia cuffietta

La Bohème was Puccini's 'coming of age' opera. Building upon the lyrical pungency and conversational style of *Manon Lescaut*, he created an iridescent jewel so meticulously fashioned and structurally balanced that it proved virtually unsinkable. We join the opera in the first act just as Rodolfo and Mimì first meet. Puccini here translates the first blossomings of love into pure sound. Each phrase, as it unfolds, is carefully shaped to reflect the natural cadences and melodic patterns of speech (notice how Rodolfo starts almost falteringly, singing the same note nine times before expanding upwards).

'How cold your little hand is,' Rodolfo tells Mimì. 'Let me warm it for you. What's the use of searching [for the candle]? We can't find it in the dark. But fortunately it's a moonlit night and she's our neighbour. I'll tell you in two words who I am, what I do and how I live. I'm a poet, I write, I live! I have a millionaire's soul with hopes and dreams of heavenly castles, but two thieves just robbed me of my treasures – a pair of beautiful eyes. They came in with you and now all my past dreams have vanished. But that doesn't matter because they have been replaced by hope!'

'They call me Mimì but my real name is Lucia,' Mimì replies. 'My story is brief. I embroider cloth at home or elsewhere. I'm placid and happy, and my pastime is making lilies and roses. I love all things that speak about love, of the spring, of dreams, and of fairy tales that have the gentle magic of poetry.'

The highlight of the virtuoso second act, with its myriad characters and multi-layered musical textures, is Musetta's waltz song 'Quando me'n vo''. What makes this passage special is the way in which Puccini gradually works in the other singers' contributions, starting with snatches of background conversation, until the whole ensemble joins in with the melody; the music surges forward in exultant waves towards a climax that comes as an overwhelming emotional release, made all the more effective by Puccini's sudden reduction of dynamic down to a mere whisper. 'When I walk alone on the street,' Musetta sings, 'the people stop, look, and inspect my beauty, examining me from head to toe.'

'Sono andati?', Rodolfo and Mimì's touching love duet sung just minutes before Mimì dies, is introduced by reminiscences of 'Che gelida manina' as a reminder of happier times. Puccini tantalisingly juxtaposes the desperate hope that Mimì may still pull through (at one point she recalls 'Mi chiamano Mimì') with a sense of forlorn, minor-key hopelessness. The duet's main theme is transformed into a funeral march at the very end of the opera as Rodolfo in anguish cries out the name of his beloved.

CD 2

Ⓦ Tosca

For all the high-impact, visceral quality of Puccini's writing during much of *Tosca*, it is the more reflective, lyrical moments that find the composer at his best. These excerpts begin with the painter Cavaradossi's little scene ('Sante ampolle!') in which the Sacristan notices the extraordinary resemblance between the person in the portrait he is working on and a woman who has recently visited the church on several occasions. Pulling a locket of his beloved Tosca from his pocket, Cavaradossi compares her beauty to the mysterious woman in the heart-stopping aria 'Recondita armonia': 'The mysterious similarities of different beauties! My beloved Floria is dark-haired. You, unknown beauty, are swathed in golden hair! Your eyes are blue and Tosca has dark eyes! Art joins the mystery of these two women. But in this painting I have but one thought! Tosca, my only thought is you! It is you!' One of Puccini's indelible melodies, constructed with repeated phrases contracting and climbing towards a central climax, is preceded by a prelude (track 2, 0:00) subtly suggestive of the painter's brushstrokes and is followed by a postlude (track 2, 2:43), the warm glow of which confirms Cavaradossi's devotion to Tosca.

The end of the first act is malevolence personified, as Scarpia reveals his true colours in his brutally menacing 'Tre sbirri'. Ordering his agent Spoletta to follow Tosca wherever she goes, he continues: 'Go Tosca! The name Scarpia is etched on your heart. Scarpia has released the falcon and inflamed your jealousy. Your suspicions offer me infinite promise! I hold two desires and the head of the traitor is by no means my most precious one. Victory is to behold the fiery passion of those eyes, and in my arms hold her languid body, throbbing with love. Tosca, you make me forget God!' Taking its lead from the oscillating pitches of two church bells, as the congregation slowly files in, the music assumes a doleful character. The whole passage gradually gets louder over the same two chords, made all the more threatening by the periodic sound of cannon fire; this creates a heightened sense of expectation resolved first in a unison E flat declamation (track 4, 3:41), which itself is then brutally swept aside by Scarpia's shattering motif (4:02).

As we move towards the end of the second act Tosca's world appears to be falling apart. Her beloved Cavaradossi has been tortured within earshot, and now in order to save him from execution she must give herself to the loathsome Scarpia. In 'Vissi d'arte' she nobly reveals the utter desperation of her situation: 'I lived for art, I lived for love. I never harmed a living soul. With a steady hand I brought help and consolation to the poor and depraved. My prayers to the above were always with sincere faith. I always placed flowers at the altar with sincere faith. Why God, in this hour of grief, do you repay me in this way?' The futility of Tosca's situation is suggested by a complete reversal of Puccini's normal practice, with each phrase falling hopelessly downwards. As the mood lifts slightly (track 5, 1:04) the orchestra recalls the music to which Tosca made her first entrance in Act I – which only serves to intensify our sense of disbelief at her current predicament.

At the beginning of the third act Cavaradossi is in his prison cell awaiting execution. Having attempted writing a letter, he lets his thoughts wander in 'E lucevan le stelle', the aria that brought the premiere to a standstill: 'And the stars were shining, and a fragrance filled the land. Her steps strode through the garden gates, her steps grazed the sand, and when her perfumed presence arrived, I fell into her arms. Oh sweet kisses, oh languid caresses, while I trembled and removed the veils from her lovely body! My dream of love has vanished forever. Time has fled, and I die in despair! And I have never loved life so much!' In an inspired moment, Puccini goes against the Italian archetype by using a solo clarinet to carry the melody right into the start of the aria, while the tenor reflects monotonally in passages of pseudo-recitative. This effectively suggests that Cavaradossi's spirit is now so crushed that he is initially incapable of converting his thoughts into melody.

ⓦ Madama Butterfly

6 Act I: Bimba, dagli occhi

7 Act I: Vogliatemi bene

8 Act II: Un bel dì, vedremo

9 Act II: Humming Chorus

The love duet between Pinkerton and Butterfly that concludes the first act of *Madama Butterfly* is not only the longest (by some distance) in Puccini's output, it is arguably the finest. This is music so full of enchantment that, like the characters before us, we feel captivated by the moment, even though Pinkerton has already made it plain (though not to Butterfly!) that he doesn't take their marriage seriously. The sheer irresistibility of Pinkerton's music (for example, the plaintive strains of the opening 'Bimba, dagli occhi') gives the audience an insight as to why poor Butterfly should give herself so freely to this utter cad, intertwining her vocal lines with his. In 'Vogliatemi bene', when Butterfly gently implores Pinkerton to 'Love me gently, gently like a little one, like a child', the fluttering of her heart is suggested by gently pulsating string syncopations.

Act I's musical continuity and ease of flow are such that Puccini denies his audience a single aria. That all changes at the beginning of the second act, when Butterfly sings the lovely 'Un bel dì, vedremo', its gentle intensity heightened by its delusional premise that Pinkerton will of course be returning to Butterfly: 'One beautiful day we will see a thread of smoke on the far horizon, arising on the sea. And then a ship appears. Then the white ship enters its port thundering its greeting. You see? He has come!' Puccini suggests the emotional duality of Butterfly's apparently unshakable faith by setting the famous opening lines to a melody that despite its cantabile sweetness is articulated by a number of uncharacteristic and mildly unsettling intervallic hops.

The 'Humming Chorus', sung as Butterfly is preparing for the long-awaited return of her beloved, is simplicity itself, the humming gently supported by pizzicato strings. Quiet and reflective, it has a tranquillity that hints at the heartbreak ahead.

10   La fanciulla del West. Act III: Ch'ella mi creda

Although Puccini may have created the new genre of the operatic Western with *La fanciulla del West*, the number that is most often requested as a separate aria and invariably brings the house down is firmly part of Puccini's world of glorious, free-flowing lyricism. Dick Johnson's 'Ch'ella mi creda' is sung just as it looks as though he is about to swing, opening with: 'I want her to believe that I'm on a new path of redemption, free and far away!' Two eleven-bar stanzas comprise this short aria, the first with the orchestra accompanying and doubling the main melody, the second (0:50) carried more by violins high above the stave. The aria's pungent, boldly etched modal harmonies and incantations look forward to *Turandot*, and made such an impression that, according to Sybil Seligman, during the First World War the Italian forces in Macedonia sang it defiantly to help sustain morale.

11   La rondine. Act I: Chi'il bel sogno di Doretta

Magda's 'Chi'il bel sogno di Doretta' is one of Puccini's most exquisite arias. Preceded by a piano introduction that unmistakably recalls Tchaikovsky's 'Waltz of the Flowers', the song is a wonderful distillation of the classic Puccini aria; it represents the apogee of the operetta tradition while pointing the way forward to the Broadway musical (albeit without the rhythmic energy) and, in the chorus, to the crooner singing tradition. 'Who could guess the beautiful dream of Doretta? Why did its mystery end? Alas, one day a student kissed her on her lips, and that kiss was a revelation; it was passion! Mad love! Mad intoxication! Who can ever describe the exquisite subtlety of such an impassioned kiss?'

12   Suor Angelica. Senza mamma

Religious operatic settings are notoriously difficult to bring off convincingly, largely because of the inherent clash between the worldly medium and the spiritual message. Puccini may not always avoid the saccharine tendency in *Suor Angelica*, yet in

Angelica's 'Senza mamma' he displays a moving restraint (considering the expressive potential of the words) that perfectly encapsulates the Sister's gentle yearning. 'Tell me, when shall I be able to see you? When shall I be able to kiss you? Oh, sweet end to all my sorrows, when shall I ascend to heaven? When will I be able to die? Beautiful child, speak to your mother like a twinkling star. Speak to me my loved one!'

The modally inflected downward phrases that characterise the main melody bear an unmistakable resemblance to those of 'Vissi d'arte' from *Tosca*, while the vocal line – sprinkled with melodic 3rds – doesn't rise and fall with Puccini's usual scalic ease.

ⓦ Gianni Schicchi

13 Firenze è come un albero fiorito
14 O mio babbino caro

Of the trilogy it is the light-hearted *Gianni Schicchi* that has emerged as a clear favourite with audiences, perhaps because it is the only one to feature anything approaching a traditional aria. The first is Rinuccio's 'Firenze è come un albero', extolling the virtues of Gianni Schicchi – and of Florence. This march-like section, clearly indebted to Bizet's *Carmen*, is characterised by lines of eleven syllables that we know from the score to be derived from the *stronello*, a poetic form peculiar to Tuscany.

The most famous passage in *Il trittico*, and for many opera-goers their favourite Puccini aria, is Lauretta's 'O mio babbino caro'. Lauretta pleads to her father with a radiant melody of such chaste simplicity that once heard it is impossible to forget. Its lyrical vein and sentimentality has made it popular in the concert hall, yet keeps it somewhat at odds with the rest of the opera's music.

ⓦ Turandot

15 Act I: Signor, ascolta!
16 Act I: Non piangere, Liù!
17 Act I: Ah! Per l'ultima volta
18 Act III, Scene I: Nessun dorma

Turandot stands at the summit of Puccini's creative achievement. Instrumentally and harmonically more advanced than anything he had written before, it shows for the first time a mastery of the epic that had until then eluded him. In *Turandot* we encounter the same fascination with violence and grotesquerie familiar from *Tosca*, only this time free of *verismo* hysteria.

We join the action during the first act where Liù is desperately trying to dissuade Calaf from attempting to answer the three riddles in order to win Turandot's hand in marriage. Puccini used pentatonic melodies so freely in his work that it comes as something of a surprise to learn that this is actually not one of his but is based on a Chinese folksong entitled *Sian Chok*.

'My lord, listen to me!' she sings. 'Liù can bear it no longer, her heart breaks! Alas, how many roads I travelled with your name on my soul, with your name on my lips! But if you have decided that tomorrow holds your destiny, we'll die in exile. He [Timur] will lose his son, and I will lose the trace of a smile. Liù can no longer bear it.'

'Don't cry, Liù!' Calaf replies. 'If a long time ago I smiled upon you, it is because of that smile, gentle little girl, that you must wait for me: perhaps you are alone in the world, but your man will come to you tomorrow.' The assembled company continue to beg Calaf to renounce his intentions to the melody of 'Non piangere' – but to no avail.

The third act features what has become the most famous tenor aria in history, 'Nessun dorma', which unexpectedly became a worldwide hit as the anthem to the 1990 World Cup. Set in a radiant G major, it is the Puccini aria *par excellence*, in which a small number of melodic shapes are juxtaposed, subtly varied, rising and falling in pitch, then repeated sequentially to create an upward surge and an emotional release. This compositional technique has been repeated countless times over the years, but rarely with such potency. 'None shall sleep!' Calaf sings. 'You, chaste Princess, from your cold room, look at the stars that tremble with love and hope. But my mystery is locked within me and no one will learn my name! No, no, your mouth will say it, when the light shines. And my kiss will dissolve that silence that has made you mine.'

The selection from *Turandot* ends with the last section of the opera that Puccini managed to complete in full score, in which Liù makes the ultimate sacrifice rather than betray the man she loves – Calaf. When asked by Turandot what powerful force lies within her heart, Liù's answer is unequivocal – 'Love!' 'I give it to you, Princess,' she continues, 'and I lose everything! Tie me! Torture me! The pain is my offering of my supreme love!' Puccini seems to have been especially compassionate when writing for Liù, perhaps another case of art reflecting real life in his operas. Just as Pinkerton's faithlessness in *Madama Butterfly* embodies the composer's own infidelities, Liu's devoted purity and suicide has clear resonances with the tragic Doria Manfredi affair, Turandot playing the role of Elvira by mindlessly crushing the innocent. Such an interpretation lends a special poignancy to a scene that was the last that Puccini completed before his own untimely death.

Index